The Power of
Positive Intention

James Peal, Ph.D.

Check Your Attitude at the Door

The Power of Positive Intention

Business Edition

James Peal, Ph.D.

Leadership Development Group

Published by Leadership Development Group
2202 Damuth Street, Suite 3
Oakland, CA 94602
Tel. 805.966.3323
www.peal.com

Cover design and typesetting by gnibel.com

Copyright 2010 by James Peal, Ph.D.
ISBN: 9780981774848
First Printing 2010
Library of Congress Control Number: 2010910800
James Peal, Ph.D., Check Your Attitude at the Door
09/2010 — 1st ed.

Table Of Contents

CHECK YOUR ATTITUDE

APPENDIX

Dedication

I dedicate this book to the key inspirations that
draw me into life, propel me through it, and make it
a rich and meaningful experience.

I

The first dedication goes to spirit.
It is where I believe we all come from; spirit is what
connects us and spirit is where we will go when we pass.
My life has one purpose, and that is to serve spirit.

II

The second dedication goes to my family and friends.
Family and friends bring me to life.
There is no greater joy than that of being a father
and sharing that joy with family and friends.

III

The third dedication goes to my business colleagues.
I thank my business colleagues for inviting me to work
with them, trusting me in that work, and collaborating
with me to create a better place to live and work.

IV

Lastly I dedicate this work to Steve Daugherty.

Following are the words I spoke to open
his memorial service.

Steve, fondly known as Dr. Love, touched all of our lives in deep, undeniable ways.

We are here to celebrate his spirit, his love, and his life. We are here to share the precious moments that we had with him and the gifts that he shared with us.

We are here to appreciate what he awakened in us, and despite his passing, to look forward to how our lives will continue to be enriched by having known him.

Steven Craig Daugherty was a true Warrior. He fought many honorable battles in his life. His battle with cancer was no less honorable.

The thing about Steve was that even if he knew this was his last battle he never wavered for a moment from being fully present with an open heart, savoring every precious moment of his life.

We know he loves his daughter, his wife, and all of us, his friends and family.

I have only the deepest respect and love for him.

After struggling with cancer for two years he died on March 9, 2010. He was forty-nine years old.

Steve Daugherty and Aria Vue

Acknowledgments

The first acknowledgment goes to you, the people who are committed to growing and developing yourselves in your lives and at work.

Special thanks go to those who have taken courses and have personally engaged in the material. Your willingness to tell your heartfelt stories, to share your personal quirks and vulnerabilities, as well as the unique things that make you tick, is inspiring. Thank you for the provocative and challenging questions, taking the tools to heart, and making positive changes in your life. Your insights, questions, and comments provide a rich and deep background that encourages and inspires. Thank you for passing your insights, knowledge, and wisdom to others.

I thank my colleagues Charlotte Milliner, Trish Barron, Simon Lovegrove, Zemo Trevathan, Lee Mun Wah, Stephen Xavier, Sherry Stucky, and Stacey LeBretton. I also acknowledge my colleagues in Germany: Hermann Mueller; the Sage Community; Ulrich Hollritt at Coralibera, for their continued inspiration and collaboration. Special appreciation goes to Charlie Sheppard, my friend and colleague. We have known each other since 1996. His generous and creative spirit has consistently sourced leading-edge models for development and corporate leadership development programs. Over the years I have worked collaboratively with the above people and companies in serving clients around the world.

Eriko Kopp-Makinose from Coralibera and Dirk Jakob from Horizonte are the co-authors of the German version of this book. Their creative energies in looking at how to make these concepts fit into German and European cultures are invaluable in producing that book and improving this one.

Ilene Segalove, my editor, has not only been instrumental in the production of this book, but has also helped me develop on a professional level; she commands my respect and thanks. I also acknowledge Carola Berger, who translated the book into German.

A special thanks goes to Dr. Roger Brum, CEO at MDSI, for his leadership and the work we have done over the years, and for challenging me to think outside of the box and be my best.

Lastly, I thank my daughter, Courtney, for the many Real Conversations we have had during the evolution of this book. I truly admire her commitment to caring for and inspiring kids and young adults to lead more aware, productive, and happy lives.

Why This Book

This book was first inspired by a corporate workshop called "Choosing Leadership." The pilot workshop was a great success and it has been adapted and rolled out to several thousands of people around the world in all types of businesses from sales and retail to biotech and pharmaceuticals, from gold mines and engineering and manufacturing plants to government agencies, educators, and students.

Many people wanted a way to deepen and reinforce their learning and share the tools they learned in the workshop with colleagues, family and friends, so this book was born.

What is New

While examples of "leadership" and "drama" are presented from models for leadership and drama, the intention of this book is for you to create your individualized and personal adaptations that have direct meaning in your life. It is important to take any model that you learn and personalize it so that it is uniquely yours. Allow the models that you learn in this book and in your life to inspire your creativity so that you can make them fit your own life.

In the appendix you will find a synopsis of some of the other the developmental background of ideas presented in this book.

Check Your Attitude at the Door complements my first book, *Daring to Have Real Conversations in Business*, published in May 2009 on Amazon. The *Real Conversations* book focused primarily on the actions you need to take to have meaningful and productive conversations at work. *Check Your Attitude at the Door* is actually a prequel to that book in that it focuses on increasing your awareness of yourself so that you can make better choices to improve the quality of every facet of your life. When you can intentionally choose your state of mind the world opens up to you in new and exciting ways.

Let's dive in!

How To Use This Book

Check Your Attitude at the Door is easy to understand and use. In no time you will learn how to pause, check in, and ultimately choose your attitude. This handy guidebook is an owner's manual that points out where the knobs are so that you can adjust your own mindset. You'll learn to see where you are coming from and what you are creating before you find yourself ending up someplace you don't want to be. Feel free to open the book in a random fashion and pick up a powerful morsel that you can use right away to make changes. Or read it front to back or vice versa. It is designed to be succinct and to the point. Take it to heart and use it as a vital motivator for real substantial attitude changes that last a lifetime.

Whatever way you like to learn, you will build a powerful continuum of skills and attitude shifts. It doesn't really matter whether or not you make leaps or incremental progress. Change will happen! Each chapter is designed to stimulate your thinking, engage your family, friends, and colleagues, and deepen your learning by providing an array of probing questions and assignments. You'll see a series of "Think About..." exercises throughout the book that encourage you to reflect deeply and often take pen in hand to answer some heartfelt probing questions. Find a notebook or journal and keep it at your side. And make sure you fill out The Check Your Attitude Pulse Check located in the Appendix to give yourself a quick assessment of your current attitude. It's a useful gauge to see where you are coming from, the impact you have others, and how you will change as you learn more about Checking Your Attitude at the Door.

> *"Learning never exhausts the mind."*
> **—Leonardo da Vinci**

Foreword: Choosing Your Story

*"We choose our joys and sorrows long
before we experience them."*
—Kahlil Gibran

We all love stories. We love hearing them and we love telling them. When my daughter was a little girl, instead of fairy tales, she wanted to hear a different story about my life each and every night. It was a way that she could learn about me and about life in general.

If you think about it there are infinite stories in the world. Some are thrillers, some are scary, others are action packed adventures or tear-jerkers, and some just really touch your mind, heart, and soul.

Events happen in your life and you make up a story about what happened. Some events are tragic by any standards; some are exhilarating adventures. If you choose to tell your story from Positive Intention, it can tickle the funny bone, touch the heart, instruct, and it leaves you and others feeling good. If you choose Negative Intention to tell your story it usually becomes a sticky drama that sucks people into your misery and leaves you and other people feeling lousy. Regardless of the events in your life, you get to choose the story that you tell to yourself and others, and you get to choose the feelings that you have about what happened.

What is the story that you're going to tell?

Here are three stories from my life that happened the first three months of 2010. They certainly took me on a wild roller coaster ride of thought and emotion. They also taught me the value and magic of experiencing life events from a positive perspective.

Mom

My mother was eighty-six years old. In May of 2009 she experienced problems with her heart. She received a pacemaker around the same time she was evacuated from her home in Santa Barbara due to a serious local fire. Shaken by the fire, she refused to return to her home, so my brother and I found a living community for her up near my house in the Bay Area. We moved her out of her house and into her new place but ten days later, she had a massive stroke. As a result, she lost her ability to speak. This would be a tragic loss for anyone, but especially for my mom because she was a Spanish professor and loved language and communicating. Over the following months, her health progressively diminished and she never really regained her ability to speak. She became very weak, and during those six months she was in and out of thirteen different facilities trying to recover.

In the final days of her life, I practiced singing "Oh Holy Night" so she could enjoy it on Christmas Eve. She was in the hospice program and on morphine. I went to her room and sat beside her and held her hands and I sang that song to her with my little iPod speakers for backup support. (I am not the best vocalist.) I sang that song and a couple of others while looking into her eyes and then told her: "You have been a good mom and have loved me and my brother and our families. Whenever you are ready to let go, God will be right here and take you up in his arms and love you forever." I thought she was kind of out of it because of the morphine, but as I went to release her hands I realized that she was holding my hands very intently and, though heavily sedated, she was actually looking at me. In that moment I kind of felt something just open up.

I don't know how to describe it, but I felt there was a clear pathway for my mother. As it turned out she passed away that night. So what I initially thought was going to be a tragic ending ultimately turned out to be a graceful and spiritual transition and completion of this life.

Donnie

A couple of weeks after my mom's passing, my good friend Clay called and said that his best friend, Donnie, whom I also knew, had just passed away. Donnie's family had asked Clay to take care of the funeral arrangements and Clay wanted my help. I was feeling totally devastated by my mother's death and inside my mind I thought, "I just can't do this, it's just too much." One evening I was over at Clay's house working on the memorial program. I still was thinking I wanted to just be by myself and not go to the funeral. But something clicked inside of me when I talked to Clay's kids and looked into their eyes. At one moment Olivia, his eldest daughter, asked me, "Well, are you going to be there at the funeral?" In that moment I felt a deep connection with Clay and his family and his wife and I just said, "Yes." When I spoke that yes something lifted inside of me. I felt energized and rejuvenated and it really, really enhanced my life to be there to help out at the funeral. I was a valuable support for other people to go through their grieving process even though I was in the middle of mine.

Steve

About a week after Donnie's funeral I received a call from Mora. She had never called me before so I knew it was not going to be good news about her husband and my friend Steve. I knew he had cancer. She told me he was in a coma and on the hospice program. She also told me that Steve wanted me to officiate at his memorial service. "WOW."Well, what an honor to be asked. It was not a matter of yes or no. He passed away a few days after her call. As long as I've known Steve, he's always been a very positive person. He turns things around and always puts a positive spin on it, and leaves you feeling really good about yourself and about life. When he found out that he

18

had cancer, it really was no different. He kept a positive attitude. Up until the very end he was planning ski trips and had me and several others convinced that we were going to Mammoth Mountain to go skiing this winter.

Steve valued each and every moment of life. He knew that he was going to die and he had actually planned his memorial. He got together with a videographer and created a two-part video that we showed at his memorial service. I have to tell you that it was one of the best services that I have ever attended. After a couple of prayers we showed part one of his video. With a big smile his opening line was, "I bet you didn't think you would see me here." The audience was rolling with laughter. After the part of the memorial where his friends spoke about him we played the last half of the video. Again with a big smile he said, "Wow, that was great. I agree with every one of you." Once again people were falling out of their seats with laughter. In the parting shots of his video he walks away, turns, waves his hand and smiles, and says, "See ya later."

His light, spirit, and love shined through! He was the radiant laser source of positive energy for all of us and while his death was untimely by certain standards, Steve met it with the greatest of elegance and honor of any human being I have ever met. I will always keep that memory of Steve alive in me to remind me to put a positive spin on things, because even when the situation is dire, I can always choose how I want to experience my life.

You can imagine that over those three months I asked myself the question, "How do I want to face my death?"

When you are facing your death, what story will you tell yourself about what had happened in your life? Will it be a tragedy, drama, comedy, or an adventure?

> *"Tragedy delights by affording a shadow*
> *of the pleasure which exists in pain."*
> **—Percy Bysshe Shelley**

Introduction

*"Anything you build on a large scale
or with intense passion invites chaos."*
—Francis Ford Coppola

Is your typical workday a serene flow of planned activities with all goals met on time? If you are making a difference at work, more than likely you are probably barraged by a myriad of decisions, details, and people that come expectedly or unexpectedly. In the background, the clock relentlessly consumes those precious moments between you and those inevitable deadlines.

While you may or may not have a choice as to *what* challenges come your way, you do have a choice as to *how* you approach your challenges. Your attitude or mindset is a choice that you make. Making this a conscious choice is what this book is about. Taking a leadership stance in this context is about being aware and intentionally checking and choosing an attitude/mindset that optimizes creativity, innovation, problem solving, and ultimately results for yourself and others.

This book is a tool box that provides ways that you can become more aware and consciously choose how you want to approach the daily events and people that come your way.

It only takes a moment to stop, check, and choose your attitude. This book is about how you can create that moment so that how you engage others creates the best impact to create results and satisfaction. The tools are brought to you through a variety of metaphors and stories from real work situations.

You will read about Mind Molecules, Mind Loops, Drama vs. Leadership, Above the Line, Checking Your Attitude, and your personal AttitudePod. There is something for everyone, whether you are the type of person who likes to crack open the book in a random flash and read a few pages or the type who likes to read from beginning to end. Practical tips, pearls, insights, and wisdom are to be gained.

Unlike the weather, your attitude is controlled by you. Like the weather, your attitude impacts everyone around you. Are you creating a threatening storm or a clear and sunny environment to work in?

While there are a multitude of attitudes and mindsets possible, for the sake of simplicity and usefulness we ask the question, "Is your attitude based in positive or negative intention?" The answer to that question becomes a self-fulfilling prophesy. Your perception of what is going on around you and how you respond is not a passive function but springs forth from decisions that you have made consciously or unconsciously.

Now is a good time to step back, become aware of yourself, and make some conscious and intentional decisions that will be the basis of how you engage at work.

"The strongest principle of growth lies in the human choice."
—George Eliot

I
Who's At The Door

1. ATTITUDE

"A healthy attitude is contagious but don't wait
to catch it from others. Be a carrier."
—Tom Stoppard

Your attitude speaks volumes before you utter a word. Like your shadow, you often are unaware of it. Your attitude permeates everything about you: the way you think, the tone of your voice, what words you choose, and even how you move your body—your body language. While you may think that your thoughts and feelings are purely private, your body is mirroring and in fact is speaking your mind. What you are thinking and feeling gets translated into your body language, and is very much like those electronic signs with a message that flashes, this time across your forehead. Your body language actually has a larger impact on others than the words you speak. Put it all together and you'll find your attitude sets the tone for how people respond to you. Everyone has experienced the vibes that come off a person. You take one look and you know whether to approach or stay away.

Barsade and Gibson consider three different types of feelings that impact your attitude, in a paper published April 18, 2007, in Knowledge@Wharton:

1. Discrete, short-lived emotions, such as joy, anger, fear, and disgust.

2. Moods, which are longer-lasting feelings and not necessarily tied to a particular cause. A person is in a cheerful mood, for instance, or feeling down.

3. Dispositional, or personality, traits, which define a person's overall approach to life. "She's always so cheerful," or "He's always looking at the negative."

All three types of feelings can be contagious, and emotions don't have to be grand and obvious to have an impact. Subtle displays of emotion, such as a quick frown, can have an effect as well, Barsade says. She offers this example: "Say your boss is generally in very good humor, but you see him one day at a meeting and his eyes flash at you. Even if they don't glare at you for the rest of the meeting, his eyes have enunciated some valuable information that is going to have you concerned and worried and off center for the rest of the meeting."

Your attitude is born out of a set of conclusions and decisions you have made about a particular person, situation, or your life. Humans like to be "right" about their thoughts and conclusions. If you have a hostile attitude you will experience hostile events in your life and approach people in a hostile way. When you are in a negative frame of mind you are sending negative signals to others and they will respond to your hostile signals in a negative way. Their response will reinforce your conclusion that the world is a negative place. If you have a cheerful attitude, likewise, you will experience events in your life in a way to support your positive conclusions. Your attitude usually resides in your blind spot because most of the time you are focused on your thoughts, not the attitude they are coming from.

For example, Frank was thinking about how much he didn't like the way that Tom communicated, but was not thinking, let alone aware, that he had a negative attitude about people who came across in a "pushy" style that was the source of his thoughts. His attitude lived in his blind spot because it was born out of automatic thinking that is the source of the thoughts that he was thinking. You are often unaware that you have "made up your mind" about a person, trait, or situation because you are absorbed in your thoughts and not observing them. Like a computer that has been programmed, your brain and habits often function on automatic pilot. Think of the computer that has just been given instructions on a keyboard. Once the "enter" key is pressed the info disappears and all you see is the screen. All the calculations are being done in the background and you just see the result. This is how it is most of the time with your mind.

Why Should You Care?

Your attitude sets the tone for how you respond to the people and events in your life. You know immediately when someone has a "bad attitude" because of the toxic environment it creates. Some people are a fight waiting to happen, or a doormat waiting to be walked on. Others are optimists or very pragmatic about how they approach life. What is your attitude toward life and your daily decisions?

How does this translate at work? Your mood impacts your performance. A multitude of research studies have been done on the impact of attitude and emotion in the workplace. Nancy P. Rothbard published a paper, "Waking Up on the Right Side of the Bed: The Influence of Mood on Work Attitudes and Performance." In her research she examines the impact of positive and negative moods that employees had at the beginning of their workday. As you can imagine, there is a direct correlation between a positive mood and work performance. People do better when they feel better. In addition, her research revealed that the mood that you have at the beginning of the day sets the tone for the rest of the day.

No one is neutral in a business. Either people are contributing toward progress or they are slowing progress. Think of someone who brings a sense of urgency with an attitude of support contrasted with someone who brings a sense of urgency with a sense of anger or threat. Who do you want to work for? Who do you want to be? If you are a boss, manager, or leader it behooves you to Check Your Attitude at the Door before you walk into work.

Your emotions are contagious. We catch them from each other especially in a confined environment such as the office. Since our relationships are predetermined by the organizational structure, we "have to" work with each other and are exposed to each other's emotions. Rank, title, and position have multiplier effects on how contagious one's emotions can be. Our bosses and leaders exert a magnified impact because of their position.

Emotional Contagion is a term that was brought to light in research done by Elaine Hatfield, Richard L. Rapson, and Yen-Chi L. Le in a paper, "Emotional Contagion and Empathy." Their research discussed the notion of "primitive emotional contagion" as one of the primary ways that humans understand, interact, and share feelings with each other. Humans have an automatic mechanism for mimicking each other on a variety of levels such as body postures, gestures, and facial expressions. When humans have similar posture, gestures, and facial expressions there will be a greater likelihood that their internal experience of feelings and emotions will "converge" or match. When someone walks into the office our systems automatically sense and respond unconsciously to what we see and hear.

Automatically and unconsciously you will tend to match the facial expressions of those around you. There is a unique connection between the musculature of your face and your feeling state. If you put a smile on your face you will tend to feel better and likewise with a frown. In one study students were taking a test; one group had relaxed musculature and the other group wrinkled their foreheads. The group that wrinkled their forehead did not perform as well on the test.

People will unconsciously mimic your facial expressions and this creates an internal feeling response that will tend to mirror yours. Smile at people and they will tend to smile; frown and they will take that cue as well. If you frown right now you will sense a different sensation internally than if you put a smile on your face. You probably just tried it, but go ahead and try it again.

Walk into the office with a scowl on your face and people will catch it from you and pass it on to others. This is not to say put a fake smile on your face. If you are feeling angry or upset and you try to smile to cover it your tension will give you away and people will feel that internal conflict as well. The only way to authentically do this is to have authentic positive thoughts and feelings. Sometimes it takes a few moments to get there but it's worth the work. In the book *Daring to Have Real Conversations*, we explain that sometimes you just have to tell your story to get out of a funk. "I was really disappointed with what happened, angry too. As I thought about it for a few minutes I started to look at what our goals are and took what happened as an opportunity to make it a lesson learned and move on." It can be very powerful to tell the story of how you went from negative to positive. That is crucial part of what it is to be a leader.

For now it is important to realize that your attitudes and emotions are not private. When you are in a leadership position – all eyes are on you and people will "catch" your emotion, mood, and attitude and pass it on to others.

Regardless of your position or title at work people are taking their cues directly from you. Your mood sets the environment that either enhances or diminishes performance for the day and may have longer term impacts. While on one hand we are all human sometimes we need to give ourselves a break. On the other hand, work is about getting results

Since your attitude makes a difference in how you and others perform, isn't it worth the investment of a couple of minutes to Check Your Attitude at the Door?

> *"A positive attitude causes a chain reaction of positive thoughts, events and outcomes. It is a catalyst and it sparks extraordinary results."*
> **—Wade Boggs**

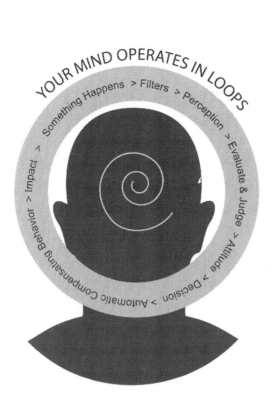

YOUR MIND OPERATES IN LOOPS

Something Happens > Filters > Perception > Evaluate & Judge > Attitude > Decision > Automatic Compensating Behavior > Impact >

2. YOUR BODY SPEAKS YOUR MIND

"I speak two languages, Body and English."
—Mae West

Whether you think you are an open book or not, you express yourself through an elaborate system of body postures, gestures, and poses. Your body is expressing or speaking what your mind is sensing or thinking. You may not know what signals you are sending, but others can read your nonverbal messages and get a lot of information about what's going on just by observing you.

Here is a story that explains how your thoughts are translated into body language:

Imagine for a moment that you are a bank teller. It's been a pretty good day but you look up and here comes someone in a bad mood. You already know he's not a happy camper. His head is hanging down. He is scowling. He walks with heavy steps, and then stops at your window with his hands on his hips. He hands you a check to deposit and then pounds on your counter, points his finger at you, and raises his voice. In only a few moments you mumble to yourself, "This guy is a real jerk."After he completes his tantrum, you make the transaction and then he turns and storms out of the bank. Although this guy is gone the experience remains. The whole scene circles around and around in your head and you hear yourself repeat, "I can't believe what a jerk that person was!!!" until you are really bent out of shape.

At this point you feel the need for some sympathy so you lean over to the teller next to you. "Could you believe what a jerk that person was?" you whisper.

And she says, "Yeah." And so it is said, "Where two or more agree, then it must be true."

A couple of weeks go by. There you are at your window on another good day, and guess who walks in the door? And what do you suppose is the first thought that goes across your mind? That is right, "There is that jerk." You make a decision. "I am going to armor up, just in case that jerk comes to my window." And sure enough, the person comes to your window. Then you decide, "I am not going to take this crap." You prepare for a fight, hold yourself upright and stiff, and quietly put on your nonverbal boxing gloves.

Today, however, that person is in a fine mood. When he walks up to the window he almost smiles, but then senses you are uneasy. He notices your scowl and crossed arms and thinks, "This teller looks like she wants to pick a fight. I better be ready for it." Then he becomes defensive and rude. And when the transaction is done, you say to yourself, "What an uptight guy. I was right. He is a real jerk." You don't realize that it was your nonverbal signals that set up his reaction.

If you have negative thoughts about the other person before you begin talking, what can you expect out of the interaction? This person is unconsciously reading your nonverbal signals and responding to them. Who is setting up whom? Who is being the "jerk"? Whose nonverbal signals are being seen and misinterpreted? Is there any chance of having a positive interaction?

This story illustrates how your thoughts are transformed into your body language and behaviors that can set up the reactions of other people. Now think about someone you have a hard time with. What are some of the negative thoughts you have about them? Now step outside yourself and look at yourself through their eyes. What nonverbal expressions do they identify in you? Is your jaw clenched, are your shoulders tight, eyes narrowed? Is the tone of your voice implying, "You idiot" at the beginning or end of each sentence?

Most of the time you are not aware of the nonverbal signals that you are sending out, yet when you see how people respond to you, you might think it is all about them. What attitude have you conveyed without saying a word?

Tony would go to the gym to work out. He was normally a friendly, outgoing type of person, but when he had a rude encounter with one person at the gym he concluded that all the guys there were arrogant jocks. He soon forgot about his generalization, but he continued to give the cold stare to just about everyone and scared people away. Tony observed people avoiding him and concluded, "Yes it's so true, they are all arrogant jocks." His perception, his attitude, was reinforced.

Jerry, on the other hand, thought everyone at the gym was better and stronger than he was. He walked with his body hunched over, and his eyes darted around and never looked anyone in the eyes. People tended to avoid him because he seemed so unavailable, and so Jerry's perception was reinforced.

Can you even identify what your thoughts are that precede your negative, possibly contentious, nonverbal signals before you even open your mouth? Are you a fight waiting to happen? Do you have "kick me" written all over your forehead? Are you nonverbally dismissing the other person? It's time to Check Your Attitude at the Door. It's time to become aware and change.

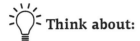 **Think about:**

1. What difference would it make if you were watching your thoughts and their patterns rather than just feeling their impact? You might think, "I see how I just labeled that person as a jerk," rather than just thinking they are a jerk and being repulsed by them.

2. What are some examples about assumptions you've made about people that turned out to be wrong?

3. Think about someone who rubbed you in an unpleasant way. Reflect on your thought and feeling patterns at the time. What did that person say or do? What was your negative interpretation? What feelings followed? What communication did you avoid in that situation?

4. Now take the above situation and put yourself in the other person's shoes. What is their experience of you?

5. When you are in a bad mood, what negative nonverbal signals are you sending out?

6. Next time you are shopping try an experiment. Notice people's reactions to you, first when you smile at them and then when you give them a blank stare. What happens?

3. THE OPPORTUNITY AT YOUR DOOR

*"Your attitude toward life determines
life's attitude towards you."*
—John N. Mitchell

You walk into each and every experience of your life with an attitude. If your personality is the climate, your attitude is like the local weather. You may be cloudy and stormy one day, foggy or sunny and bright the next. Your attitude not only flavors and colors your experiences of other people and life, it sets the tone for how others experience you. Most of the time, you are not aware of your attitude.

Unfortunately, many people treat their attitude just like the weather; they assume it is totally out of their control. Do you? How often do you operate on autopilot and yet unknowingly assume you are just being yourself? Because you may not be aware that you can choose your attitude, you often take the cards that are dealt to you by your unconscious reactions and long-term habits and don't think twice. "This is who I am," you claim. "This is what I have to do." But it's just not true. You have a choice to Check Your Attitude at the Door and wake up.

Your Life Is A Reflection Of Your Choices And Your Attitude

Do you feel like you are the innocent recipient of whatever comes your way? Does it feel like life just dishes out experiences? If you want to know about the choices you have made, just look at your relationships, work, home, and how you feel about yourself right now. Listen to that little voice in your head. What is your commentary to your life? Are you living up to your potential or is something just not right? Does life seem unfair? Are anger, disappointment, and sadness core themes to how you feel? Do you feel something is missing? How do you get a handle on things to start turning your life around so that it is moving forward in a direction you would prefer? There is no need to just throw your hands in the air. There is no need to give up. Do you recognize and feel like you are in charge? Well, you are.

You are the creator of your life experience, not a passive recipient. Each moment of your life, every experience you have gives you the opportunity to Check Your Attitude, yes, at the door, to check to see what you are thinking and, in so doing, what you are creating. The goal is to enter into life with your eyes, ears, heart, and mind open, aware of what you are creating and how you are creating it. If what you are experiencing is not what you want, then you stop for a moment and intentionally reset your attitude and shift to an experience that is going to benefit you and those around you.

If you want to Check Your Attitude, look at what is happening in your life and what is happening around you. What do you see, hear, and feel? What is the dialogue going on in your head? By paying attention to your experience you will learn a lot about your mind and the choices you are making.

What do you see in this picture? Do you see someone celebrating or someone flailing? You don't need to be a psychiatrist to interpret your perceptions; you can do it for yourself. Whatever you see in front of you is always a reflection of your thinking and your attitude. If you see someone celebrating, you are in a positive frame of mind. If you see someone flailing, you either are flailing yourself or you are looking for someone who is. Are you ready to embrace the challenge of living fully? Are you ready to create a positive impact in your life and in the lives of others? The degree to which you engage in life is the degree to which you can truly lead rather than take a back seat. If you are ready to make that commitment, then you are ready to turn the page and step into an exciting and exhilarating way of living.

Have you ever watched or listened to somebody who is really, really good at what they do? They make it look so natural and effortless, don't they? Often you wonder, "Why do they have this easy life and I have to struggle?" You don't see the amount of pain and frustration they have had to go through. You watch a dancer and tend to forget the hours upon hours of practice and failure they've had to survive as they craft their art. And so it is with creating your life. Most people want to take a shortcut. Most people want to feel others are lucky and they aren't. It's easier to just blame others or feel sorry for yourself. It's so much easier than activating and going after what you are passionate about.

Malidome Some, a spiritual teacher, says that when you are on your true path in life you will experience great obstacles. He goes on to say that our spirits like to be clever and create a way to success when things seem impossible. When you are up to something great, you will have great challenges to overcome. True expertise and success always require a vision, hard work, a clear direction, and a conscious commitment to achieve excellence. You also need to include knowledge, solid tools, and practice, practice, practice.

"Nothing can stop the person with the right mental attitude from achieving their goal; nothing on earth can help the person with the wrong mental attitude."
—Thomas Jefferson

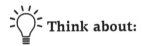 **Think about:**

1. Take a piece of paper and draw a vertical line down the middle. On the left side write down all the things you don't want in your life. For each of those items ask yourself, "If I didn't have that, what would I want to have in its place?" Write your answer in the right column. Use the right-hand answers to set the direction of your life.

2. If you were to fulfill your dreams and goals, what would your life feel like? How would others experience you? How long do you think it will take you to achieve what you want to achieve?

3. At the end of your life what do you want to say about your life? How do you want to feel about the life you lead?

4. Who are the people that you admire the most? What are the qualities you see in them? How do you emulate those qualities? How can you add some of their qualities to your personality and behavior?

5. Ask someone you trust how they perceive you. Ask them directly, "What are my positive strengths and weaknesses or blind spots?" Ask them what they have learned from being around you.

6. Think of a positive change you have made in yourself at home or at work. It need not be a huge shift. How did you make that change? What makes a change long lasting for you?

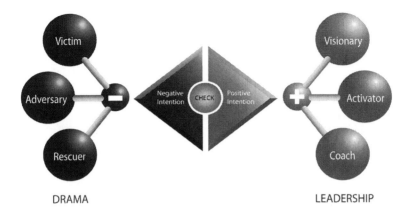

DRAMA   LEADERSHIP

4. MIND MOLECULES

"You don't have a soul. You are a Soul. You have a body."
—C. S. Lewis

Rather than thinking of your mind and body as who you are, consider the following two perspectives:

1. Think of yourself as the author or the artist with the pen or brush and your mind like the paper, a place where your thoughts, ideas, and choices come together for your perception. As the author or artist you choose what goes on the canvas of your mind. You get to choose the color of ink, the words, ideas, images, and feelings that get expressed on the canvas of your mind.

2. As a scientist your mind is where you generate idea molecules that form your experience of life. You can create molecules that have a positive charge on them or molecules that have a negative

charge. When you create thoughts based in Positive Intention you are making mind molecules that have a positive charge. Mind molecules are unique because they attract like molecules.

Choosing positive intent attracts other like elements to that nucleus of positive intent and you will build a molecule that has certain positive unique characteristics. When you choose Positive Intention, you will tend to move yourself into the future to see your vision in life, how to activate your vision, and how to support people around you.

Positive thoughts have a positive impact on your body and your physiology. "When you have good chemistry with someone, your body produces elevated levels of the neurotransmitter norepinephrine," says Helen Fisher, Ph.D., research professor of anthropology at Rutgers University. When there's true chemistry, the body's levels of the chemical dopamine rise and lead to "imprinting," a theory of attachment discovered by German ethologist and Nobel Prize winner Niko Tinbergen. Ever notice when you have good chemistry with someone the world seems brighter? This could be due to a physiological reaction discovered by University of Chicago biopsychologist Eckhard Hess, a pioneer in the area of "pupillometrics." In short, Hess found that when people look at something or someone that causes positive feelings or sparks interest, their pupils dilate in an attempt to take in more of it, letting in more light as well. You go into an enhanced physiological state when you are in a positive frame of mind.

A Yale and Miami University study tracked the lives of people over fifty for twenty-three years and found that those who embraced the aging process lived an average of 7.5 years longer than those who were pessimistic about getting older. Other studies reveal that optimists are not only less likely to die from heart disease, but if they do happen to develop it, recover considerably faster from coronary bypass surgery than their negative counterparts.

Though there are no clear explanations for the health benefits a positive outlook brings, scientists believe there is a solid link between optimism and the immune system, providing it with the boost it needs to fight the pitfalls of aging and disease.

Conversely, if you choose negative intent, that negative charge will attract other negative elements to form a negative molecule around the nucleus of negative intent. When you choose Negative Intention, you will tend to be looking at the past, where you feel victimized, angry, and in need of rescuing. Your body responds to your negative attitude by making your breathing shallower, tightening up and slowing your metabolism. You have less oxygen going into your system when you are in a negative state of mind. The main chemical that's overproduced by negative emotions is adrenaline. This hormone is produced by our bodies to give us the ability to defend ourselves or to run away from danger. When you are in a negative state of mind you are typically feeling threatened in some way. Adrenaline heightens your hearing, vision, smell, and taste, and gives you amazing short-term strength and stamina. The next day, when there is no danger, you feel sluggish, your musclesache, and your joints hurt... an adrenaline hangover.

Chronic stress from negative attitudes and feelings of helplessness upsets the body's hormone balance and depletes the brain chemicals required for positive feeling. New scientific understandings have identified the pathways through which human emotions, such as hope and fear, impact the body's immune system and overall vitality.

Your mind is not a two-dimensional canvas or piece of paper; your mind is a holographic device that displays a lifelike hologram of reality. If you have seen the later versions of *Star Trek*, your mind is like the "Holodeck," a holographic room on the *Enterprise* that is lifelike and that you, the operator, program. Your mind creates your personal internal version of reality for you to experience. This hologram is so realistic that it is often mistaken for reality itself and you forget that you are the author of the contents of your mind. When you step into the Holodeck you experience what seems to be a real situation. Each person's internal reality is what I will refer to later in this book as a bubble of experience. Inside of your bubble is where you get to experience your version of reality.

The great thing is that each and every moment provides you the opportunity to choose what type of energy and experience you want to create and have. That choice is what this book is about.

> *"What we call the secret of happiness is no more*
> *a secret than our willingness to choose life."*
> **—Leo Buscaglia**

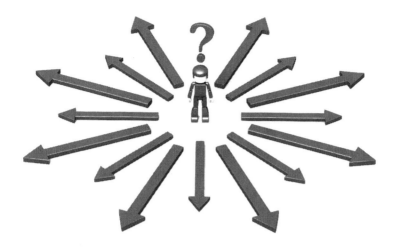

5. CHOOSING IN THE MIDST OF CHAOS

"Chaos is the score upon which reality is written."
—Henry Miller

So often you rush through life reacting to an onslaught of ever-changing people and situations. Rather than taking a breath and reflecting on what you are doing or, more importantly, how you are thinking, you fall into automatic pilot or end up spinning into a blur of experiences. Wouldn't you prefer to choose how you feel so that you can respond rather than just react to the many challenges of your work and personal life? By Checking Your Attitude at the Door you can stop and seize the moment to become more present and conscious.

As a human you are inevitably sitting smack-dab in the middle of a barrage of sensory information. There are a multitude of triggers in your environment that send you into all kinds of thoughts and emotions. It is great when these are positive influences, but at times you get caught in the undertow of negativity. Sometimes these negative thoughts and emotions become habituated and automatic. I am sure you have encountered someone you might identify as a "negative" person. For these "negative" people, much of their thinking and feeling is unconscious. They are like a sailboat that has no captain. No one is manning the sails and they float wherever the wind, dark waves, and strong tides take them. Why not be at the helm of your experience as well as in touch with your internal rudder so that you can steer your life in the direction you want to make intentional positive mental and behavioral changes? Through awareness and practice you can become the captain of your attitude and set sail into a fulfilling life with intentionally conceived positive mental behaviors and actions.

It may be optimistic to believe in the inherent fundamental goodness in each person, but what is the alternative? Sometimes it takes a little work to tap into that fundamental level of positivity. Sometimes it takes more work to see that positivity in others. But if you don't make that effort, you become part of the problem, not part of the solution. Rather than trying to change people (an impossible task) learn what to do when you find yourself in a negative frame of mind and you want to turn things around. Giving the benefit of the doubt is choosing to operate from Positive Intention.

When you operate from Positive Intention more possibilities and choices become available to you and those around you. Conversely, when you operate from Negative Intention you lock yourself into a rigid I'm right/you are wrong frame of mind that tends to alienate others and limits growth, creativity, and good will. As you build a foundation of positive intent you will get a chance to take a good look at your own mental thought patterns, your emotions, and how you impact other people. You will also become astutely aware, if you haven't already, that awareness by itself is not enough to change. Just like an athlete in training, it takes work to gain a level of ease and expertise. You will have to work at building a new attitude, but the payoff is a more satisfying life, one where you exhibit more control and freedom, regardless of what situation you find yourself in.

This book gives you the information and inspiration you need so that you can choose your attitude no matter the circumstances, with positive intent and the ability to act with confidence instead of reacting with negativity, avoidance, or confusion.

It's all about learning how to be aware, Check Your Attitude at the Door, and then choose the attitude that serves you best.

> *"Every man builds his world in his own image.*
> *He has the power to choose, but no power*
> *to escape the necessity of choice."*
> **—Ayn Rand**

II
Be Aware

6. THE 3 PRINCIPLES—
AWARENESS, ATTITUDE,
ACTION

"The ancestor of every action is a thought."
—Ralph Waldo Emerson

It all starts with your thinking. Your thinking is the primary source of all of your choices. Addressing how you think makes it possible to produce the results you really want. Here you will find tools to enhance your **awareness**, tools to cultivate a positive **attitude**, and guidance on how to take the right **action**.

As you increase your awareness you will begin to understand how your mind works and how your attitude impacts your thinking, emotions, and body language. This understanding enables you to come from positive intent, builds a positive attitude, and inspires you to take the actions in your life that will make a difference. Your actions, in turn, reflect your choices that build awareness and feed your attitude. Positive Intention builds momentum that spirals upward and improves your life and the lives of others. Destructive loops, based on Negative Intention, spiral downward and diminish your life energy and the world around you.

Each and every moment provides you with the unique opportunity to make meaningful choices. Each of your choices creates a unique future, yet most of the time you enter into life unconsciously, simply triggered by what is around you. You respond in an often knee-jerk fashion without rhyme or reason. The truth is you can manifest the kind of experience you want to have. It is up to you. As you enter into each experience, you stand at a door. It's a significant place of choice. Checking Your Attitude at the Door means that you pause for a moment, reflect on your choices, and then intentionally choose to have a positive impact.

Life is meant to be lived forward, not backward. When you assume Negative Intention you are facing your past and living a life of trying to avoid what happened. You can imagine what it might be like if you drove your car backwards only using your rearview mirror! When you try to avoid negative experiences you keep your attention on what is negative. If I tell you not to think about a green elephant with yellow polka dots, your mind has to think of the elephant first in order not to think about it. If you want to give a presentation and you are thinking, "Don't be nervous. Don't be nervous," your mind has to think about being nervous first. It is much more powerful to think, "Feel confident." Use the compass of Positive Intention to set the direction of what you truly want in your life, and with awareness and a clear attitude take action in that direction.

"You only live once, but if you do it right, once is enough."
—Mae West

7. THE BUBBLE YOU LIVE IN

"Get your facts first, then you can distort them as you please."
—Mark Twain

You live in a bubble of experience. Even though you may look like every other human being from the outside, your experience of life on the inside is completely unique. No one experiences life EXACTLY the way that you do. Most people do not realize that they inhabit their own personal bubble of experience; they assume that the bubble is reality rather than their perception of reality.

Now that could seem like either a lonely place to be or a great opportunity to learn about yourself and others. Once you understand how your bubble of experience is created and sustained you will have greater freedom to understand and get along with other people. Once you realize that you are experiencing a very sophisticated hologram that is created by your senses, you can begin to have some freedom to become the architect of your life.

THE LAYERS OF YOUR BUBBLE

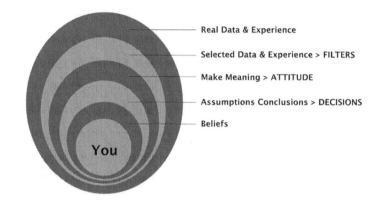

Peter Senge refers to the Ladder of Inference in his *Fifth Discipline Fieldbook.*

- Your nervous system is very much like a holographic video camera that records everything, The Real Data & Experience.

- Next you select snippets of Data & Experience with a sophisticated Filtering system to create what you are actually aware of.

- Once you become aware of something your system Makes Meaning of the selected input by comparing it to past experiences and thoughts.

- Your Assumptions and Conclusions are born out of taking several past experiences and pulling them together.

- Your Conclusions become embedded over time and become the foundation for Beliefs.

- Beliefs are a deeper set of conclusions that you have made about yourself and the world.

- Your beliefs create the basis for your actions.

- In addition, your Conclusions and Beliefs contribute to the Filters you use to Select Data & Experience.

- This is a circular type of arrangement because once the Conclusions and Beliefs are in place you selectively notice parts of your incoming data that will reinforce your beliefs.

- As your nervous system matures these patterns become part of your automatic way of perceiving and acting in the world.

How long does it take your nervous system to go through all of those calculations? Blink your eyes— about that long. Your mind is that fast. And the real issue is your conclusions aren't always in alignment with what is really going on outside of you. That's how blind spots are created. What you believe isn't always what is.

RICK'S TOTAL BLIND SPOT[1]

Rick Ross tells a story of how he misread a situation that revealed a big blind spot in his thinking:

> I stood before the executive team, making a presentation. They all seemed engaged and alert, except for Larry, who was obviously bored out of his mind. He turned his dark, morose eyes away from me and put his hand to his mouth to cover a yawn. He didn't ask any questions until I was almost done. Then he interrupted with: "I think we should ask for a full report." In this work culture, that typically means, "Let's move on."
>
> Everyone started to shuffle their papers and put their notes away. "Larry obviously thinks that I am incompetent," I muse—which is a shame, because these ideas are exactly what his department needs. Now that I think of it, he's never liked my ideas. Clearly, Larry is a power-hungry jerk. By the time I've returned to my seat, I've made a decision: "I am not going to include anything in my report that Larry can use. He wouldn't read it, or, worse still, he'd just use it against me. It is too bad I have an enemy who's so prominent in the company." In those few seconds before I take my seat, I have gone through a set of assumptions, attitudes and feelings that often lead to misguided beliefs.

---

[1] Excerpt from *The Fifth Discipline Fieldbook*. Copyright 1994 by Peter M. Senge, Art Kleiner, Charlotte Roberts, Richard B. Ross, and Bryan J. Smith.

Look at what happened to create Rick's big blind spot on a journey that took less than a second:

- Rick noticed Larry yawning and looking dark and possibly critical. He did NOT notice that Larry was listening moments before.

- He winced when Larry demanded a full report.

- He assumed Larry was critical of him.

- Next he concluded that Larry thought he was opposed to him.

- Lastly he started plotting against Larry based on all of the above "information" (misinformation) and the cycle is complete!

- This is Rick's Total Blind Spot.

"It all seemed so reasonable, and it happened so quickly, I wasn't even aware I'd done it," says Rick about jumping to numerous conclusions that were off the mark. Or were they?

What was not evident in the above story is that Rick already had a belief that he was a poor presenter. This began in the eighth grade when he gave a speech in front of the room and the teacher criticized him while the entire class laughed. Personal history plays a huge role in how your bubble is constructed and what you notice and think about. It also contributes to the evolution of your blind spots. You don't see what you don't want to see on some unconscious level. Or you see things that really aren't there based on your historical pain and prejudices.

It takes an intentional effort to catch yourself in this process. Most of the time you can only reflect on what has happened. This is when you Check Your Attitude at the Door. Yes, opening your mind and awareness is the passageway to identifying old patterns and new possibilities. When you close your mind and your awareness you lock yourself into known patterns that will eventually lead you into a rigid way of thinking, feeling, and behaving.

Some people are locked in their little bubble and some experience an ever-expanding bubble that is permeable to the world around them. How does it happen that some people are locked inside and some are free? It is a function of how they think. Assuming negative intent about people and the world around you locks you in your bubble. Assuming Positive Intentions will open up possibilities and expand your world and make you a person who can contribute something to this world.

*"Adopting the right attitude can convert
a negative stress into a positive one."*
—Hans Selye

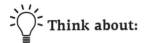 **Think about:**

1. What have been the significant positive and negative experiences in your life?

2. Describe a negative experience in your life. Here are some pointers to help you paint a more complete picture:

   a) The Event: What were the real data and experience? To clarify, if you were a neutral observer, what were the facts?

   b) What parts of the event stand out in your mind?

   c) How does this event compare with other similar events?

   d) What meaning did you make of it by comparing it to past experiences and thoughts?

   e) What assumptions and conclusions result from taking several past negative experiences and "bucketing" them together?

   f) What conclusions have become embedded over time to become the foundation for your beliefs?

   g) What beliefs did you form from these conclusions?

   h) How do you now act based on your beliefs? Notice how those beliefs are now part of the filters through which you perceive.

8. SEVEN PLUS OR MINUS TWO

"Common sense is genius dressed in its working clothes."
—Ralph Waldo Emerson

Seven to ten billion bits of information are streaming into your nervous system RIGHT NOW and in each and every moment! How do you process this onslaught? How do you decide what to focus on and what to forget or put on hold? Your nervous system is designed to "make sense" of all of this input and create a smooth and stable experience. But it does that at a cost. You end up ignoring much of what is going on and selectively paying attention to only parts of your moment to moment realty. This is how you maintain your sanity, or at least what seems like sanity. Of course, it is impossible to be aware of everything.

Your plate is full; in fact, overflowing, and more than likely you are running through the events of your life on auto-pilot. Yet in the midst of this barrage of chaotic input you make endless choices that impact the quality of your life and the lives of those around you. Are you aware of what your choices are? Are you aware of the choices you have made today? Your life is a collection of the results of the multitude of choices that you make every second. While you can't be consciously aware of every choice you make, you can be selective about the choices that will impact you the most. If you are like most people, you don't realize that you are actually the author, creator, and sustainer of your attitude and experiences in life. Most of the time you probably have the sense that you are the spectator and recipient of experience rather than the creator. Most of the time choices seem to be made for us. But each moment you can choose to be and act from a positive state of mind or a negative state of mind. This is a huge choice. It defines who you are; it defines your basic attitude about living.

9. BLIND SPOTS

Since billions of bits of information flood into your nervous system every second, you can only imagine that you'd have to have some blinds spots. Can you imagine what it would be like if you were actually consciously aware of everything streaming into your senses? That is a lot of information! Think about the wide-open look on the face of an infant whose nervous system is totally open to all the millions of bits. "Seven to ten million bits...I've got to sleep...I am tired...I am hungry...Someone change my diaper...I need a break." No wonder they sleep so much!

As your nervous system developed, it formed two aspects of awareness. One part is your conscious mind, very much like the tip of an iceberg, floating above the vast, usually shadowed, other part, your unconscious mind. Your conscious awareness is like a spotlight. It shines a light on something specific, something particular happening in this very moment. Right now for instance, you are aware of the words on the page, perhaps you hear the sounds in the room, but you are probably not aware of what your tongue is doing. Ah, now you are. That is because the word triggered a specific part of your conscious mind to focus on your tongue.

You can choose to direct your spotlight of conscious awareness to different parts of your experience. In the process you can build a stronger muscle of awareness that allows you to discover, identify, and actually shrink your blind spots. This requires becoming more and more receptive to paying attention to what is going on in the moment.

There are verbal and nonverbal clues about what is happening, and you need to recognize them first and foremost. Once identified you can re-educate your awareness to be open and alert to seeing and using all of the feedback available, not just the tiny pieces you usually focus on.

Tony was a manger of a process improvement group. One of his direct reports, Sandy, shared his strategic approach and they viewed their business in a very similar fashion. Naturally they would fall into an easy rapport with each other in hallway conversations and in one-on-one meetings. Tony wasn't aware that in regular team meetings others viewed this rapport as favoritism. When leading a group he would unconsciously and consistently ask Sandy what she thought more often than he would engage with others. Although unintentional, his behavior revealed a blind spot. He was unaware of how he acted and how he was perceived.

"Who looks outside, dreams; who looks inside, awakes."
—Carl Jung

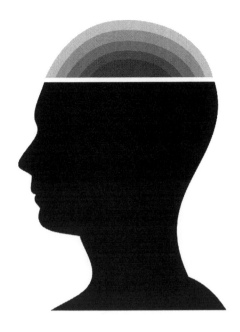

10. WHERE DID YOU PUT YOUR AWARENESS?

"Ignorance is no excuse, it's the real thing."
—Irene Peter

Awareness can be elusive, and yet without awareness it is very difficult to change. Awareness is actually the key that allows you to consciously shift your behavior from making lucky or accidental changes to *intentional* changes. Awareness allows you to take possession of your choice points and leads you toward a clearer focus of what you want. Through clarity you can then take positive action.

Science explains how awareness works by delving into the anatomy of the brain. Basic awareness of one's internal and external world, called phenomenal awareness, originates in the **brain stem** in the center of the brain. "Higher" forms of awareness called "access awareness," including **self-awareness** and language, require the involvement of the cortex, which wraps around the surface of the brain. Access awareness makes information in your mind accessible so that you can express it verbally in a reasonable fashion. It also affects how you control your behavior and awareness of both introspection as well as memory (e.g., something that you **learned in the past**).

The tools in this book are intended to build greater levels of awareness so you can see your patterns, witness your thinking, and identify how you create and construct your reality. Through awareness you will become more and more able to "see yourself" and recognize your patterns of perception, your various attitudes, and your behaviors. With awareness, you can also better understand what triggers you into nonproductive loops of thought and feeling.

Awareness is the first step toward making a tangible change in your life. Without it, change just becomes happenstance. You may bump up against an experience or have something traumatic happen and this creates the impetus for change. However, the purpose of this book is to stimulate intentional change through awareness so that you can be the architect of your life.

WHERE IS YOUR AWARENESS?

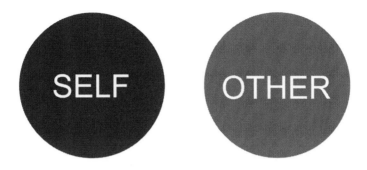

You can focus your awareness in three distinct dimensions:

1. SELF: Awareness of your internal thoughts and feeling processes; awareness of your body language.

2. OTHER: Awareness of how another person is experiencing you and their thinking/feeling process.

3. OBSERVER: Awareness of the interaction from a neutral or observing point of view.

Cheryl took a leadership course that builds awareness. She was given an exercise where she recalled a misunderstanding she had with a co-worker. Cheryl went through a practice dialogue and then needed to focus her awareness on the three distinct dimensions of awareness: Self/Other/ Observer. First she became aware of her internal thoughts, feeling processes, and body language (SELF). Cheryl found it easy to identify her limiting beliefs about the other person. She thought the other person just wanted to be right, didn't want to receive any input, was being stubborn, and was threatened by Cheryl's tenure. She could also recognize how completely justified she felt in her perceptions about the other person's behavior in the situation.

Cheryl was then asked to step out of herself and to sit in the other person's shoes (OTHER). When she looked back at herself through that person's eyes, she was able to see how she (Cheryl) was coming across and began to understand that she (Cheryl) was actually being stubborn. She could also see from the other person's shoes that she was being antagonistic and difficult because she (Cheryl) did not think she was being heard.

Cheryl then stepped outside to the neutral point of view (OBSERVER). It was now clear to her why she was having this pretend misunderstanding. She could see the dynamics at work without feeling attacked or defensive. She saw what was lacking in the communication between her and her co-worker and recognized she had more options than she thought. "Yes," Cheryl said, "I can handle the problem with clarity now."

By stepping into and exploring each of the three distinct dimensions of awareness (self-other- observer), Cheryl gained new insights into solving the dilemma. She realized she could learn to listen better and also could see how her body language was off- putting.

Emotional Intelligence, a concept and book by Daniel Goleman, states that awareness is an important part of an individual's emotional intelligence. Somebody who has a high degree of emotional intelligence is able to shift their awareness intentionally and automatically into the three dimensions of awareness: self, other, and observer. Developing mastery of awareness increases your emotional intelligence. Somebody who has a high degree of emotional intelligence is able to shift gears in between the three dimensions of awareness. They can freely go into the self position, they can step into the shoes of the other person and they can also step outside the situation and look at it from an observer's point of view very much like shifting gears in a car.

Ted was angry about the house being a mess when he came home from business trips. He thought that his wife, who was home all day long, should be able to clean up and have the house neat for his arrival. He began to build up resentment toward his wife and felt that he could not broach the subject due to her defensiveness about the topic. When he stepped into the self position he could see his adversarial thoughts and attitudes. When he stepped into her position he realized that she did not feel appreciated for all the other things that she was doing, primarily taking care of the kids. When he stepped to the observer position he could see the whole relationship and realized that he needed to be more complimentary in his communication with her.

Perhaps you are more prone to be self-aware or to be aware of the other person, or maybe you are one of those people that assess the situation naturally. Whatever your strength is, the goal is to increase your awareness flexibility by either stepping into the other person's shoes, stepping into the observer's point of view, or stepping into your own shoes and exploring and developing your awareness in each of those positions. This is something that you can do alone in preparation for interactions with others, as well as during the actual interactions and conversations.

You can practice this skill with friends while you are talking. Shift your attention to being in their shoes and look back at yourself. Then step outside and look at what's happening in the interaction from an observer's point of view. In these types of casual settings, you can build your awareness so that when you find yourself in more critical types of settings, your awareness will automatically shift into the three different dimensions. Although you may display more strength in one of the above areas, the more that you can become fluent in all three, the greater degree of freedom you will have in your interactions to create the results that you want.

MASTERY AND MATURE AWARENESS

Mastery means that you are able to build a mature sense of awareness. Mature awareness means that you are present to observe your own thoughts and feelings without the knee-jerk desire to either dismiss them or slip into autopilot. You can actually pause, check, and reflect on what you are going through first. You can become an observer of yourself. This can be uncomfortable at first. Or you may see something about your attitude you don't like and you want to make a change immediately. But acting in haste under these circumstances often causes you to make another choice that ends up creating just as much, if not more, discomfort or confusion.

Mastery means that you have the ability to be with and feel your choices, without flinching or falling into a default mode. You learn to breathe, relax, feel the moment, and then choose positive intent. This type of change is not about instant transformation. It is one that comes from genuine self-examination, self- acceptance, and a clear idea of where you are going and what it is that you want to do.

"It is the mark of an educated mind to be able to entertain a thought without accepting it."
—Aristotle

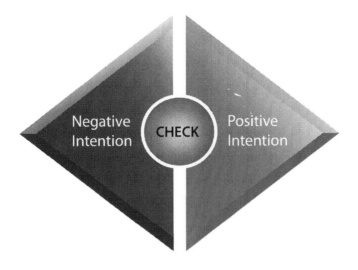

11. INTENTION AND IMPACT

"Action speaks louder than words but not nearly as often."
—Mark Twain

Your intention refers to your specific purpose or desired goal. Intention is what motivates your actions. Your intention is independent of whether or not the action will produce a successful or unsuccessful impact. Impact is what other people experience as a result of your behavior and/or actions.

You can understand more about the relationship between intention and impact by examining the following illustration. Four quadrants define how your intention and impact interface with one another to cause different effects. Depending on what your intention is and the impact that you have, your behavior will fall into one of these four quadrants.

—If you have Positive Intention and a positive impact, it is called authentic behavior.

—If you have Positive Intentions for others in a situation and have a negative impact, that is called missing the mark. Your intention is good; however, your behaviors don't create the impact that you desire.

—If you have Negative Intention and create a positive impact, this is labeled manipulation. Basically, you fool people into believing you, but you actually have a hidden agenda for your exclusive gain.

—If you have negative impact and Negative Intention, this is sabotage. Sabotage may be overt or covert, but typically it is covert. In other words, the other person doesn't have an awareness of what your intentions are, yet you are able to have a negative impact on them.

Positive Intention

Miss the Mark	Authentic
Sabotage	Manipulation

Negative Impact (left axis) — Positive Impact (right axis)

Negative Intention

Most of the time when you operate from Positive Intention your motives are either overt (made clear) or there is transparency to them. You will either tell the other person up front what your intention is, or you will answer honestly when asked. There is nothing hidden. When people operate from Negative Intention they typically keep their motives covert (hidden). When somebody tries to make you feel good or does something positive just to take advantage of you, they usually will not tell you their intention. Likewise, when somebody says or does something to ruin you, they usually will keep their intention a secret.

Sabotage Scenario:

Frank had a negative perception of his boss and felt that she was selfish and out for her own good. Consequently, on several occasions when topics would come up in meetings, Frank chose to keep information to himself rather than share with the group and his boss. Consequently, his boss had a great deal of difficulty dealing with situations that came up because she did not know everything she needed to know. This resulted in her consistent failure at solving the problems at hand. This is a good example of sabotage. Frank had a Negative Intention and a negative impact.

Missing the Mark:

Roger wanted his team to work well together. When issues came up in staff meetings he would look at the person in charge and say, "Fix it." Sadly, this strategy did not work because more discussions needed to happen to move things forward. In this case, although Roger's intention was to empower the person to take care of the problem, it really didn't fulfill its purpose. His team needed him to interact further in problem solving. Roger had a good intention and thought he was empowering his team, but his communication had a negative impact.

Manipulation:

Steve felt that he always had to get people to do what he wanted. In meetings he would tend to have an overbearing way of steering the conversation toward his outcomes. He believed that the team wasn't quite capable of coming up with the right decision. After a meeting his team usually felt they had wasted their time because Steve had already decided the result and generally disregarded any feedback. His use of manipulative tactics created frustration. "Why didn't he just tell us what he wanted rather than pretend he wanted our input?" they would comment. The consensus was that Steve had a hidden agenda.

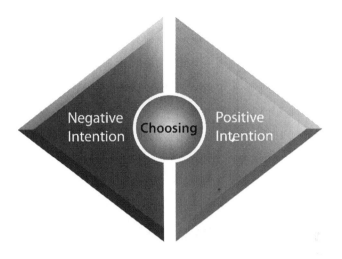

12. CHOOSING POSITIVE INTENTION

"There is little difference in people, but that little difference makes a big difference. The little difference is attitude. The big difference is whether it is positive or negative."
—W. Clement Stone

When you choose Positive Intention you instantly engage with the world. Your bubble becomes more permeable and you have more access to the people around you. Self-acceptance and appreciation of others become your foundation. When problems arise you look toward a solution and take action. Connection, compassion, and contact are possible.

When you come from Positive Intention you speak the truth and you feel an even, easy flow of energy.

In the simplest of terms, you always have the choice to speak or not speak the truth. If you are not speaking the truth, for the sake of simplicity, you are lying. Your body comes with a built-in barometer for knowing when it is telling the truth or not. That is right, you are actually built to know how the truth feels. When you are coming from Negative Intention, there is a palpable distortion or fragmentation in that energetic flow. When you hear someone lie, you know it; maybe not in a verbal way, but something shifts inside of you. Yes, truth and lies express themselves as physical sensations that can be read and evaluated.

Think about a time someone told you or you told someone a lie or bent the truth. Remember how it felt? Do you feel a tension as you think about it? Do you feel a sinking sensation in your gut? How about a surge of adrenaline or agitation or a kind of anxiety or panic? Your body actually responds to the memory of those kinds of disconnected, uncomfortable sensations.

When you choose Negative Intention you cut yourself off and see others through your lens of criticism and judgment. Your permeable bubble hardens and little touches you because you are on the attack or are being defensive much of the time. Negative Intention creates the hard shell and all you can see are your own negative assumptions. You literally shut down and find yourself inhabiting a world of false assumptions, worries, what ifs, and oh no's.

Positive Intention connects you. Negative Intention isolates you, and out of fear you pass up the opportunity to make vital communications. Negative Intention is certainly not the best place to come from if you want to make growth-oriented decisions or create reasonable, compassionate, or real conversations. It is crucial to learn how to come from Positive instead of Negative Intention. Thinking and operating from Positive Intention is the foundation for moving through your doubts and fears and allows you to enter into the kind of attitude that serves everyone. While it all starts with your thoughts, it all ends up in your actions.

Getting To Positive Intention:

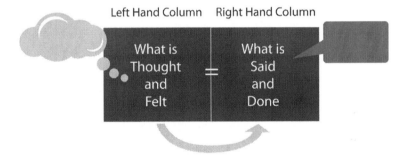

Left Hand Column   Right Hand Column

What is Thought and Felt = What is Said and Done

WHAT IS IN YOUR LEFT-HAND COLUMN?

Peter Senge, an author on personal mastery in business, created a useful model called the Left-Hand Column, which helps you understand more about building a positive attitude. Here's how it works. Think of a recent important interaction that you had. Now draw a line down the middle of a piece of paper, creating two equal-sized columns. Under the left-hand column, list all of the things that you thought, felt, and wanted to say in your conversation, but did not. In the right column, list what you actually said. Finally, ask yourself, "How do the two columns compare? Is there a significant discrepancy?"

Look at the example below:

Tom's Left-Hand Column	Tom's Right-Hand Column
There is no way we can ever achieve that. How ridiculous. You are an idiot!	"Hmm, you bring up an interesting point."

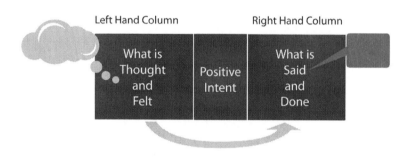

As you consider what is missing, you are actually building awareness of how to create more positive intent. Operating from Positive Intention is about achieving some sort of equality between what is in your left-hand column— what you think and feel— and what is in your right-hand column—what you actually say. Obviously, you aren't going to utter every thought in your mind, but in order to have a meaningful interaction you need to make sure you express what is important during your actual exchange. The next chart illustrates the addition of a Positive Intent column to show how you can transform your thinking into speaking, and a new right-hand column to show how the communication changed.

Tom's Left-Hand Column	Positive Intent	Tom's New Right-Hand Column
There is no way we can ever achieve that. How ridiculous. You are an idiot!	This person is thinking outside the box. They are being very creative. They want to stimulate discussion.	Help me connect the dots here. I am not sure how you arrived at your solution. What was your thinking? How did you come up with that solution?

"Do you know the difference between education and experience? Education is when you read the fine print; experience is what you get when you don't."
—Pete Seeger

RAISE THE FLAG EVERY DAY

Living Positive Intention has been described as raising a flag every day, but there is no place to tie it. Practicing Positive Intention requires intention, attention, and expectation. As you commit to operating from Positive Intention, expect that you will be given many opportunities and repeatedly challenged to maintain that positive attitude. As long as you can expect to be challenged, you can use the challenge, embrace it, and learn more about yourself and increase your mastery. Positive Intention is not a destination; it is an evolutionary spiral that enhances life. Again, you will have infinite opportunities to Check Your Attitude and change your thinking and actions. Grab them and practice raising the flag.

As with athletic training, you might feel a little sore when you begin, but with practice you will gain a level of expertise and actually create the experience of Positive Intention for yourself and for others as well.

GUT CHECK

Your first response to challenging events and situations is one gauge to measure your progress and level of mastery. How do you feel? Be as aware of your thoughts and feelings as possible. When you build this level of vigilance from a non-judgmental place it will help you make great leaps. Simply notice your mind, thoughts, and feelings without knee jerking yourself into a reaction. This pause and attention will build your ability to make Positive Intentional choices about your life. Check Your Attitude and become an active observer of your mind. It will instantly help to neutralize negative reactions.

PRACTICE 3 STEPS TOWARD POSITIVE INTENT

1. Acknowledge your first thought.

2. Suspend Negative Intention and seek Positive Intention.

3. Frame your situation and formulate a good question that you can ask the other person to engage him or her in dialogue.

Jamie has a way of bragging about herself. She often talks about her role in things and what she accomplished to the exclusion of promoting other people or people around her. Every time Tim would hear her front page herself he would cringe and regret his association. In this situation Tim decided to pause for a moment and ask himself, "What is she trying to do by promoting herself?" After some thought he realized that she needed to be acknowledged and that she was doing it for herself because she did not hear it from the outside. Two things happened for Tim after he had that realization. One was when he heard her acknowledging and boasting about herself he had a neutral reaction, and from time to time he would actually compliment her on the work that she did. In this situation Tim changed from wanting to be right about how wrong she was for self-promotion to understanding her situation and actually contributing to a solution. Everyone likes to be acknowledged anyway.

This practice works to transform how you approach difficult situations. It may seem awkward at first, and it may feel like it's not the right thing to do. This sensation is resistance. When you assume Negative Intention, your mind wants to be right about how wrong others are. This is an effective time to push the pause button on your negative thinking so that you can create the possibility for a positive result to occur.

Your mind has been conditioned to be right at the expense of making others wrong. Often you may think, "Well, that person is wrong and I am obviously right." Even if you are right, a problem develops when you need to point out that she is wrong and insist that you are right. This one-up-manship creates a hostile environment. To shift the interaction to the possibility of having Positive Intention you need to ask yourself, "How do I lead her to this result or conclusion in a way that she is going to feel OK?"

You will have to practice assuming positive intent over and over until it becomes a natural way of thinking and acting. Do not expect it to happen automatically, but in time you will easily shift your thinking, and you will be amazed at the results as you find yourself engaged in potent dialogues and interactions that change and improve everything you say and do.

Emotions have a Positive Intention. Look at the chart below to get a sense of what the Positive Intention could be for disappointment, anger, and stubbornness. In addition to the Positive Intention there is a column giving a few tips on how you might approach someone in that emotional state.

Emotion	Emotion - Process	Positive Intent	Engage them by..
Disappointment	Is let down by an expectation that is unfulfilled.	Has high expectations and is committed to results.	Acknowledge the goal he/she wants to accomplish. Reassure in your confidence in his ability to achieve.
Anger	Something is not going as expected. A defense for the fear of losing something, or failing.	The person knows what they want. Has a lot of energy and focus. Has a sense of urgency.	Convey your understanding of his/her goal. Ask about the concerns and what steps can be taken to mitigate.
Stubbornness	Resistant to change.	The person wants to be certain that results can be achieved in new direction.	Ask for what criteria needs to be fulfilled in order to shift. Ask about concerns.

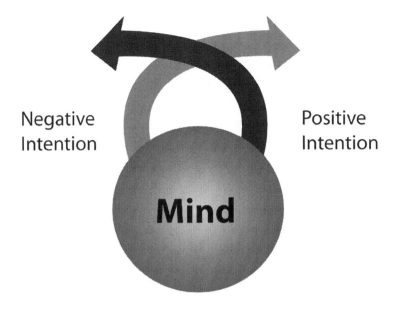

Negative Intention

Positive Intention

Mind

13. THE POSITIVE INTENTION OF NEGATIVE INTENTION

"There is nothing so pitiful as a young cynic because he has gone from knowing nothing to believing nothing."
—Maya Angelou

Now that you know more about how to assume Positive Intention with other people, you need to understand how your internal defense system works. Then you can apply the practice of assuming Positive Intention with yourself. Once you understand the shortcomings of defending yourself you can take yourself to the next step of creating something positive. Assuming Positive Intention toward yourself is a major step toward leading a satisfying life.

Your body and mind are designed with a multitude of defense mechanisms to protect you from harm and danger. If you touch something hot, you pull your hand away. Likewise, if you cut yourself your body sends white blood cells to attack and dispose of the harmful bacteria that might infect you.

Neil Neimark, M.D.,[2] explains that when we experience excessive stress—whether from internal worry or external circumstance—a bodily reaction is triggered, called the "fight or flight" response. Originally discovered by the great Harvard physiologist Walter Cannon, this response is hard-wired into our brains and represents a genetic wisdom designed to protect us from bodily harm. The fight or flight triggers chemicals like adrenaline, noradrenaline, and cortisol to be released into your bloodstream. Your respiratory rate increases, your pupils dilate, your awareness intensifies. You become prepared physically and psychologically—for fight or flight.

We scan and search our environment, "looking for the enemy," notes Dr. Neimark. *"Since you tend to perceive everything in your environment as a possible threat to your survival your fear can be exaggerated and your thinking distorted. In our homes and offices, as civilized as you may appear, it is possible to feel threatened and often you may feel trapped, trying to control yourself while stewing inside."* If it seems like someone is harming you or about to harm you, your mind takes a stance to protect you from that negative impact. You will label that person as negative in an effort to create distance and/or safety.

---

[2] Neil F. Neimark, M.D., www.TheBodySoulConnection.com, 2010

There are a couple of flaws in the human mental defense system:

1. It is based on your perception of the other person's intent, which may have nothing to do with their actual intention. You often will imagine or assume Negative Intention because this person is acting like someone else out of your past even though their intention may be totally different.

2. A defense system is based on avoiding something negative rather than creating a positive result or taking positive action.

3. The moment that you assume Negative Intention, you imagine a future of that person doing damage to you. This thought automatically creates a bad feeling regardless of whether or not that person will actually do any damage to you in the future. In this way you are inflicting that damage upon yourself.

Joe has strong assumptions and perceptions about Shirley. He thinks, "Oh, she is just out for herself and doesn't care about me. I have to hunker down when I am around her." Joe imagines Shirley will act in a way that will exclude him and possibly harm him in the future. This makes Joe feel bad about her, and he carries that bad feeling around to remind himself to keep protecting himself. The problem is that Joe has to experience that bad feeling every time he thinks about or is around Shirley. This may actually be worse than the damage that she might do if his imagined scenario were ever to come about. The defense mechanism is trying to protect but is actually hurting Joe. You cannot have a positive experience when you are in a defensive mode.

When you notice you are defending yourself:

1. Stop for a moment and question your thoughts of Negative Intention. Ask yourself, "Do I really think this person is out to ruin me?"

2. Identify the Positive Intention of your defense mechanism. Ask yourself, "What am I trying to protect myself from?"

3. Substitute a positive way of thinking and acting. Ask, "What are some other ways I can think about this situation?"

In the above situation Joe may have had the experience that Shirley acted in a way that did not seem to take his interests into consideration. Upon reflection Joe understands that his defensiveness was a protective device. He just felt he was not being heard. Once he got that he could assume Positive Intention and replace the thought of, "Oh, she is just out for herself and doesn't care about me," with, "I can take care of my own interests." This switch to Positive Intention in how he perceives the situation gives him many more options. For example, Joe can now enter into a dialogue with Shirley to discover her intentions rather than just assuming she is out for herself, or he could choose to change the situation altogether and look for other people to interact with where he has a natural affinity.

Frank was in a long-term relationship. In this relationship his partner was always grilling him about where he was and what he was doing every minute of the day. Underneath the questioning was a suspicion that he was having affairs with other people. Frank was annoyed by the constant barrage of questions and did not know what was fueling them until the end of the relationship. In his next relationship his partner started asking him about his whereabouts when they were not together. Frank automatically felt annoyed again, just as he had in the previous relationship. Frank did not realize that the new person was just curious about his life and not suspicious of anything at all. For months Frank carried a negative feeling about the new person's questions that had nothing to do with the new relationship. It was not until Frank questioned his own internal defensive reaction that he realized that he was defending himself against mistrust and that what he really wanted was to have a trusting relationship. Then he was able to approach his partner from a positive place when asking about her intention.

Think about:

Reflect on a troublesome or unpleasant situation with another person at work or in a personal relationship.

1. What was the negative commentary inside of your head about the other person or people? What did you assume about their intention?

2. What were you defending yourself from? How were you trying to protect yourself from this person?

3. What could be a Positive Intention that you could have for yourself instead?

4. For each of the above situations, think about/create the Positive Intention for the other person or people.

5. Craft a response based on positive intent.

III
Know Your Attitude

"Change is inevitable—except from a vending machine."
—Robert C. Gallagher

Increasing your awareness is an ever-expanding life practice. This means there will always be something new to discover, even in the final breaths of this lifetime. This section provides you with tools that you can apply to improve the quality of your work and your personal life by developing more awareness about your attitude and how you can check it at the door.

The best way to gain mastery with the many skills presented is to *prepare, practice, and participate.* Many people find that keeping a journal of notes is a good way to reinforce learning. Writing is a powerful way to prepare and start the process because it helps you absorb concepts and make them your own. One form of practicing is to verbalize your thoughts and ideas out loud. Sometimes repeating what you are thinking out loud can help you become more aware of your thought patterns. Practice what you want to say out loud so you can hear it. Also looking in a mirror and saying what you need to say can be a way to practice. Once you have prepared and practiced it is time to participate. When you go into the world, well, this is truly where the rubber meets the road. You will be able to watch how your mind operates to intentionally create responses and successful outcomes.

The focus of this part of the book is to help you recognize what state of mind you are in and provide tools to enhance and build upon your strengths. The skills that you will learn are organized around recognizing when you are in a negative state and how to turn it around and operate from Positive Intention.

One level of mastery is when you are able to Check Your Attitude, recognize you are in a Negative Intention Molecule, and intentionally shift into the Positive Intent Molecule. Once you are in the Positive Intent Molecule, the next level of mastery comes through strengthening your positive qualities, being a role model, and being in service to others.

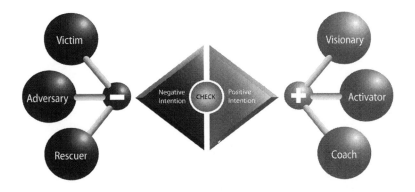

14. THE MIND MOLECULES

Your mind makes many different types of experience molecules. In the following chapters you will be looking at two examples of classic molecules based on positive and negative intention. By looking at these examples you will be able to reflect on your own process and the types of molecules you have created in your life and the types of molecules you will have to intentionally create.

The elements that comprise the two molecules represent six fundamental attitudes you can have in life. They have been given names of types of personalities to make them easier to grasp. Of course these are not purely separate and you will see that the three points in the Positive Intention Molecule are related and conversely the three points in the Negative Intent Molecule are related as well. If you are familiar with the Karpman Triangle you will see the similarity with the Negative Intention Molecule. Likewise, if you are familiar with the Leadership Is a Choice™ or Choosing Leadership materials you will see a similarity of the Positive Intention Molecule with the Leadership Triangle.

You can think of two realities that exist simultaneously, one positive and one negative. You can live in a state of Negative Intention/Drama or you can live in a state of Positive Intention/Leadership. You get to choose which one you want to live in and that choice exists for you in every moment.

Each molecule is self perpetuating. That means your choice of Positive or Negative Intention will create either a constructive or destructive molecule that reinforces itself and will attract and/or create other molecules like itself. Your mind is very much like a computer. Your mind does not care what program it is running, but the program you create will determine the quality of experience that you have. If you choose Positive Intention you will feel more like being at the core of your strength. If you choose Negative Intention you will probably feel more like you are in quicksand.

Every scientist uses the periodic table of elements when making a molecule. You can start with any element and build a molecule. You can also look at which elements with a positive spin you want to make stronger in your life. In the appendix are short definitions and descriptions of the elements and the Positive Intentions of the negative spin elements.

Check Your Attitude® Periodic Table

									Sv — Service
Sb — Sabotage									
Vt — Victim	Re — Resigned	Bl — Blame	Dr — Drained	Sp — Suspicion	Tr — Trust	Pa — Passion	Cm — Commitment	In — Inspiration	Vi — Visionary
Ad — Adversary	Df — Defensive	Ag — Anger	Fs — Frustrated	At — Attack	Eg — Engaged	Cr — Creativity	Hu — Humor	Ac — Accountable	Av — Activator
Rs — Rescuer	En — Envy	Ha — Hidden Agenda	Su — Superior	Ar — Arrogance	Ap — Acceptance	Em — Empowers	Tp — Transparency	Cf — Confident	Co — Coach

Negative Spin   **Choice**   **Positive Spin**

vi·sion·ary

Date: 1648

1: having or marked by unusually keen foresight and imagination

2: able or likely to see a future goal or condition that may seem unattainable or impractical from the perspective of today

3: able to see what is coming when there is not any present evidence

Step back and look at the big picture, where you are going, the final destination. Deal with details and remember to look at things from a higher altitude.

THE STRUCTURE OF THE MOLECULES

The words that interconnect the elements of molecules represent the key emotions and experiences that are associated with each molecule. They are arranged to mirror equivalent experience for each molecule; i.e.:

Negative Intention — Positive Intention
Resigned — Inspired
Blame — Commitment
Drained — Passion
Suspicion — Trust
Defensive — Accountable

Anger — Humor
Frustrated — Creativity
Attack — Engaged
Envy — Confident
Hidden Agenda — Transparency
Superior — Empowers
Arrogance — Acceptance
Etc.

CHECK YOUR ATTITUDE SCORECARD

The score card can give you a quick at a glace to check where your attitude is. See the score card and questions in the appendix.

CHECK YOUR ATTITUDE SCORE CARD		
RATING		**SCORE**
Suspicion -5 -4 -3 -2 -1 <> 1+ 2+ 3+ 4+ 5+ Trust		____
Blame -5 -4 -3 -2 -1 <> 1+ 2+ 3+ 4+ 5+ Commitment		____
Angry -5 -4 -3 -2 -1 <> 1+ 2+ 3+ 4+ 5+ Humor		____
Drained -5 -4 -3 -2 -1 <> 1+ 2+ 3+ 4+ 5+ Passionate		____
Arrogance -5 -4 -3 -2 -1 <> 1+ 2+ 3+ 4+ 5+ Acceptance		____
Resigned -5 -4 -3 -2 -1 <> 1+ 2+ 3+ 4+ 5+ Inspired		____
Defensive -5 -4 -3 -2 -1 <> 1+ 2+ 3+ 4+ 5+ Accountable		____
Hidden Agenda -5 -4 -3 -2 -1 <> 1+ 2+ 3+ 4+ 5+ Transparent		____
Envy -5 -4 -3 -2 -1 <> 1+ 2+ 3+ 4+ 5+ Confident		____
Frustrated -5 -4 -3 -2 -1 <> 1+ 2+ 3+ 4+ 5+ Creativity		____
	TOTAL SCORE:	____

15. POSITVE AND NEGATIVE INTENTION

POSITIVE INTENTION MOLECULE

*"It takes but one positive thought when given
a chance to survive and thrive to overpower
an entire army of negative thoughts."*
—Robert H. Schuller

Positive Intention opens you to possibilities and forward movement. The three points on the Positive Intention molecule work together. The Visionary sets the direction or goal, the Activator determines the process of how to get there, and the Coach supports the people. You have all three elements inside of you and will have particular strengths and weaknesses in each area.

In the Positive Intent molecule you have everything that is necessary for the creation of what you want in life. The Negative Intent Molecule is the place where destructive cycles and habits get created and maintained.

Let's take a look at some of the key relationships that make up a Postive Intention molecule. The visionary sets the vision and where we're going. Between the visionary and the activator we have the quality of creativity. The activator forms the path to the vision and does this in a very creative way. The connection between the coach and the visionary is one of confidence. The coach works with people so that they can feel confident in achieving the vision, achieving the goals. Between the activator and the coach there is trust. The coach instills a sense of trust. The activator instills trust in terms of making it to the goal by providing the pathway. As we look at how these three elements—visionary, activator, and coach—connect with the nucleus of Positive Intention we see that the visionary brings in the quality of passion and commitment. The activator brings in the level of accountability and humor. The coach brings in a sense of empowerment and transparency.

> *"Positive anything is better than negative nothing."*
> **—Elbert Hubbard**

NEGATIVE INTENTION MOLECULE

"The only disability in life is a bad attitude."
—Scott Hamilton

As we look at the construction of the drama molecule—the victim, adversary, and rescuer—the victim's relationship to the rescuer is one of being powerless. The victim feels powerless. The rescuer sees the victim is powerless and is there to save the day. The relationship between the victim and adversary is one of anger and attack. The victim feels attacked by the adversary, and the adversary is angry at the victim for creating the failure and blaming the adversary. Between the rescuer and the adversary there's a since of suspicion. Neither one trusts the other's intentions. As we look at how these three elements connect with the nucleus, victims feel drained and resigned. Adversaries are defensive and frustrated, and rescuers feel superior and they have a hidden agenda. You can take any one of these individual elements in and of itself if you focus on it enough you'll actually attract all the other elements to make a negative intention molecule.

THE DRAMA CYCLE

The Adversary is the attacker, the villain, the one who likes to blame the Victim. The Victim plays the helpless one who is at the mercy of the Adversary. The Rescuer is a false hero and wants to save the Victim from the Adversary and the Adversary from her own vengeance. Each of the roles can shift very quickly from one to the other. You can be Adversarial in one moment, and then feel Victimized in the next. The Negative Intent Molecule is sometimes known as the Bermuda Molecule because it sucks the energy out of all relationships in a flash. These roles can encompass departments or leadership groups as well as individuals.

In this section of the book a thumbnail description of each of the six points on the molecules is provided along with key descriptors for each point.

For the Positive Intention Molecule there is a section that relates the Strengths Finder themes for that point. Marcus Buckingham's book, *Now Discover your Strengths*[3], along with the online assessment tool, is a great resource and a worthwhile investment. You can use the online assessment tool to identify your strengths and your leadership style in any situation.

The Victim is persecuted by the Adversary and the Rescuer tries to save them both. More specifically, the Adversary projects his flaws onto everyone else and sees himself as faultless. The Victim projects her power onto others, and then claims to be helpless. The Rescuer projects his sense of uselessness onto others so his can feel that he is needed.

You can see that the three elements, the Victim, the Adversary, and the Rescuer, are all part of the thinking that feeds Negative Intention. Victims assume negative intent about themselves and believe that the world is going to take advantage, punish, or hurt them. Adversaries assume negative intent in terms of being right and assuming that others are wrong, and Rescuers see the world as a helpless place needing their support and salvation. These roles become symbiotic, forming one big vicious cycle, and each of

---

[3] *Now Discover Your Strengths*, Marcus Buckingham, Donald O. Clifton. New York : Free Press, 2001. StrengthsFinder 2000, 2006-2009 Gallup, Inc. www. strengths.gallup.com

these points becomes a kind of support for the other two. This is a very depleting self-perpetuating drama.

The Negative Intent Molecule is a quicksand pit created by the Victim, the Adversary, and the Rescuer. The Victim will grab hold of you and drag you down with him. The Adversary will tell you it's your fault for getting into the quicksand, and the Rescuer will throw you a rope but not tie it to anything or hold onto it, making it impossible to really get out.

> *"I've learned that people will forget what you said,*
> *people will forget what you did, but people*
> *will never forget how you made them feel."*
> **—Maya Angelou**

16. RECOGNIZING YOUR PERSONAL DRAMA

THE NEGATIVE INTENT (DRAMA) MOLECULE ISN'T PRETTY

"The moment there is suspicion about a person's motives, everything he does becomes tainted."
—Gandhi

NEGATIVE INTENTION

When you are coming from Negative Intention you shut down and your bubble of awareness turns into a thick shell that constricts you. You only see and hear your own thoughts and feelings. When you are in Negative Intention you are convinced that you are right about what you perceive and feel. The Negative Intent Molecule is where you abdicate responsibility for your life and begin to project negative qualities on yourself, others, and the world. When you operate from Negative Intention your world also seems like it is filled with people who are negative. You put a negative spin on the events in your life as well as on what people say or do.

Carol worked for Debbie for many years and they developed a deep level of trust and partnership. For some reason over the past six months Debbie became suspicious of Carol's intentions. In the middle of a project Debbie began to make unusual requests of Carol. Although Carol had always notified her of project meetings, Debbie now insisted on attending them, although she had rarely done so in the past. This shift required Carol do a lot more work and rescheduling. "She is micromanaging me," Carol proclaimed, and she believed she was not being given the space and freedom that she was used to. In addition, Debbie wanted to review and edit all of Carol's outgoing project emails. Once again, Carol felt resentment about this new behavior.

When Carol brought up her concerns, Debbie responded, "I am not being any different. I don't know what you are reacting to." Their relationship began to deteriorate and communication became strained. Despite their prior agreement not to handle conflicts over email, they got into an email exchange, which only made things worse. Each person was left to interpret the other's mail from a negative point of view. They fell deeply into the Negative Intent Molecule.

Carol felt victimized by Debbie's new behaviors and became adversarial. After conversations with Debbie, things only seemed worse for Carol. She could not get over the feeling that she was not trusted. Debbie felt that Carol was attacking her unjustly and could not understand why. This led her to believe that Carol was trying to undermine her. The relationship was strained for months.

Finally, Carol and Debbie worked with a coach who helped them sort out their thoughts and feelings. They worked hard to assume renewed positive intent about one another. Their following meeting was much more productive as they both got to tell their own story and also were open to listening to the other's experience and perceptions. Carol and Debbie were playing different roles in the Negative Intent Molecule. Once they identified their nonproductive personality traits they could finally make some positive shifts.

You will be way ahead of the game if you can honestly identify how you play the three roles in the Negative Intent Molecule as you interact with people. If you deny that you ever operate from this place, you are fooling yourself. Face it, everyone has nonproductive personality traits, and the sooner you admit it, the easier it will be to create other, more useful choices.

Use the following descriptions of the Victim, Adversary, and Rescuer to help you identify which role you play when you are in the Negative Intent Molecule. Ask yourself which situation, people, or behaviors trigger you to be in the drama as well.

In addition to relating to these classic personalities, notice your personal variations on the theme. Perhaps you will come up with one, two, or three elements that comprise your personal negative intention molecule. Roles may include Saboteur, Pessimist, Helper, Skeptic, Guilty, Fault Finder, Jealous, Fatally Flawed, and a host of others.

VICTIM

"Self-pity in its early stages is as snug as a feather mattress.
Only when it hardens does it become uncomfortable."
—Maya Angelou

Victims have betrayed their own value by not believing in their own self-worth.

Mitch had an open-door policy, and people were always coming into his office. Many used his couch as a place to complain. He would listen patiently. No matter the work piling up on his desk or the fact that this visitor was regurgitating the same problem over and over. He nodded his head and hung in there. Inside his own mind, though, he'd complain about this person and how he couldn't really get his work done because his time was being monopolized. Mitch didn't want to be rude. When Mitch finally got to his staff meetings, he would rant about how people kept coming into his office and taking up his time. He went on about how he had to work extra hours and how exhausted he was. Despite the advice his peers gave him to close the office door, he'd always say, "Oh, no, no, I can't do that. I have to be there and be available."

In this situation, Mitch played the Victim. He simply refused to do anything about his situation and would just complain ad infinitum. This behavior is characteristic of the Victim. They whine about what's happening to them without taking responsibility for their behavior directly contributing to the perpetuation of what they claim they don't want.

When Mitch got home from work he was inundated with requests from his loved ones. "Would you get this for me?" "Can you help me?" Although he was exhausted and needed a few minutes to recharge before tackling home tasks, he ignored his needs and did everything for everyone else. In his mind he felt drained but felt he "had" to serve. Instead of telling those around him he needed fifteen minutes to chill out, he secretly resented their requests and guzzled down a beer or two to calm down. Later he would complain to one of his buddies about all the pressure he was having at work and at home.

Victims start with the premise that they are helpless and powerless. Right off the bat they just give up. Victims assume that everyone else or some other entity has the power and they have no control; life happens to them. They truly have the experience of not being in control, and they do very little to affect or control anything about their life situation or circumstances. Victims feel that everything around them is a threat because they think they have no power. They also feel betrayed by people's actions and lack of consideration. Victims also put themselves in the place of being wronged or violated. They have a lot of unspoken rules and a lot of unspoken lines that get crossed. If someone looks at them the wrong way they interpret that person as hostile, and even that look will victimize.

A Victim is like the kid who goes limp when you want to pick him up. Suddenly he is terribly heavy and you can't do anything with this helpless lump that has rubber legs and can't walk on his own.

A Victim's need for approval, for acknowledgment, for recognition is never satisfied. No matter how much she gets she is always going to find a place where it was missing, a place where she wasn't noticed. Or she'll say, "Yeah I got acknowledged this time but the last five times I wasn't acknowledged." Victims are always testing those around them by covertly and subtly seeking approval, and when they don't get it they feel justified in having a lesser view of themselves. They feed their own victimhood and are in a continual loop of complaining and being disappointed with life. They have an attitude of being inferior. Victims project all the positive qualities outside of themselves onto other people and internalize the negative qualities and the self-diminishing qualities. Victims are drained of energy because they don't have a strong enough core of positive thoughts about themselves. They have betrayed themselves and betrayed their own value and their own worth by projecting it all onto other people.

When a problem arises a Victim says to himself, "It is hopeless and I am helpless," and this will reinforce and justify him doing nothing about it. Because he see himself as incapable of doing anything directly, he feels that he must placate the world. If he is angry about something, he will not express it directly. He will instead become passive-aggressive. Victims are plagued with excuses of why they can't do something. They will complain, "It is because the process won't let us. It is because so and so did this to me. I don't have enough time." They are victimized by their circumstances and by other people. Their passive-aggressiveness and lack of energy often frustrates others because it comes off as covert and sabotaging.

Victim

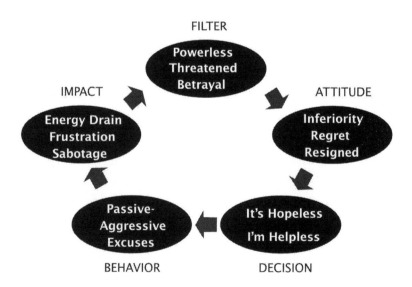

128

When you are around a Victim it is an energy drain. Victims have their internal cycle of being powerless, but they won't ever recognize or acknowledge their own power, and this creates a black hole. Victims don't intentionally take energy from you; they think their energy away and think that others have what they can't have. When you connect with their world you will feel the same energy drain that they do.

> *"Pessimist: One who, when he has*
> *the choice of two evils, chooses both."*
> **—Oscar Wilde**

HOW YOU THINK WHEN YOU ARE IN VICTIM

- I am helpless.
- I have no power to change this.
- _____ took away all the choices.
- I can't do this because ____ is stopping me.
- It won't work.
- It is too late.
- My time has passed.
- Someone else has "it"; I don't.
- I don't count.
- I am worthless.
- ____ (excuse) is making me perform poorly.
- What I think or feel doesn't count.
- I am less than _____
- This is not my decision, but I have to go along with it.

- They made me mad.
- I just had to sit there and take it.
- They pressured me into saying yes.

Victims simply resign themselves to external factors and say:

- "Well, there's really nothing that I can do about it."

- "That is just the way it is and I can't really do anything about it."

- "There is nothing I can do to change it."

YOU ARE IN VICTIM WHEN:

1. You blame outside circumstances for your situation.

2. You do not see yourself as powerful; you feel you have to take the cards the way they are dealt and have no choices.

3. You often think that other people have positive qualities and you do not (jealousy and envy).

4. You have excuses for everything.

5. When you have an issue about someone you do not talk with the person directly. Instead, you ei-

ther create negative gossip or complain to someone else.

"Action cures fear, inaction creates terror."
—Douglas Horton

STRATEGIES TO NEUTRALIZE YOUR VICTIM WAY OF THINKING

- Do a review of your strengths. Write them down. Ask yourself what differences they have made in your life.

- Identify the negative spin you put on events.

- Identify where you give your power away to a person or situation.

- Identify the shoulds, can'ts, and have to's you always say. What rules or false beliefs keep you stuck?

- Begin to say "I want to" or "I choose not to."

- Most people who feel victimized by their circumstances do so by saying, "I can't leave because..." Realize you are not trapped but are unwilling to face the unknown. Accept that you choose the current situation and in so doing are not trapped by it.

- Have a conversation with whoever you have issues with.

- Own the fact that you have given up on yourself and that you can't expect someone to make up for your lack of self-worth; only you can make yourself whole.

- Forgive those who you think have betrayed you. Forgiveness is giving up your right for revenge forever.

- Realize that regardless of what happened, what someone said or did, it was your perception and interpretation of it that has made you feel bad and continues to make you feel bad.

- Realize that you have internalized a negative thought about yourself that is not true.

- Recognize that you are, at your core, good.

- Forgive all the people in your life who have said or done mean things to you.

- Realize that you are feeling sorry for yourself rather than doing something to change your situation.

- The change you want will come when you change your thinking rather than waiting for someone else to change.

"You can't be a victim and heal."
—A. J. Langer

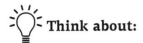 **Think about:**

1. What situations or people trigger you into the Victim mode?

2. What do you say to yourself when you are in the Victim mode?

3. Take one or more of the Victim Neutralizers and write out the answers.

4. What other elements might you substitute for the Victim that fit for your experience? What negative emotions and attributes are related to your personal elements?

"If it's never our fault, we can't take responsibility for it. If we can't take responsibility for it, we'll always be its victim."
—Richard Bach

ADVERSARY

"It is a very rare man who does not victimize the helpless."
—James Baldwin

Adversaries blame the world as a defense rather than taking responsibility for their own shortcomings.

THE MICROMANAGER ADVERSARY

Stanley was one of the principles in a small software company. He was a detail-oriented person and often found mistakes in other people's work. Consequently, he had a perception that people weren't quite doing enough and certainly weren't living up to his expectations. As a result, he would even more intensely scrutinize and critique the work of his direct reports. Usually he bypassed anything that was done correctly and went right to what looked wrong. He would then point out all of the mistakes to his direct reports, adding his specific directions on how they were supposed to fix each and every problem.

Naturally, Stanley's direct reports felt excruciatingly micromanaged, under attack, and demoralized by his management style. Of course, Stanley felt justified since his people weren't quite cutting it and he knew he needed to be hard on them.

Because of his negative perception of his employees' work, Stanley took on an adversarial role. Rather than engage in training or instructing his team, he simply kept them focused on following his instructions and intervened by bossing them around.

When Stanley got home from work he would nitpick and fuss about all the things in the house that were not working perfectly. His family rarely felt appreciated because of his constant barrage of criticism. If anyone approached him he would ask if they had finished the task that he had assigned to them. He was usually in a bad mood and very temperamental. When his kids came with grades from school, he always asked them why they didn't get higher scores. His kids were doing well in school but never felt like they were good enough because of Stanley's adversarial approach.

THE ANGRY ADVERSARY

Brenda always spoke in sharp and abrasive tones to her team. Whenever they would come and ask her a question she would snap back, and they would recoil. Nobody really enjoyed a conversation with her because she always seemed to be hostile. Brenda was tightly wound, red faced, and even had veins bulging on her forehead. Inside of her mind, though, she felt surrounded by incompetents. That forced her to be disappointed, angry, and on edge, always pushing and snarling for them to get things done the right way.

Adversaries always focus on what is wrong. They point the finger outside of themselves and are very critical, looking for who is at fault. They often will acknowledge what is wrong or what is missing but not acknowledge anything positive. Adversaries put themselves in a one-up position, and naturally that means everyone else is below or less than. They come off as condescending, with an inflated self-image, and are often seen as arrogant. Adversaries' one-up position supports their anger about how inferior the world is around them. They are always looking outside of themselves for fault because they see themselves as faultless.

When you are around an Adversary, you feel attacked. They express their hostility directly or often through sarcasm. They will typically take a defensive posture when criticized or asked to take responsibility. Adversaries make people feel pressured, intimidated, and just plain wrong.

Adversary

FILTER

What's Wrong Criticism Fault Finding

IMPACT

Make Wrong Pressure Hostility

ATTITUDE

Condescending Arrogant Outraged

Attack, Blame Sarcasm Defensive

I'm Right You're Wrong

BEHAVIOR

DECISION

HOW YOU THINK WHEN YOU ARE IN ADVERSARY

The Adversary looks outside themselves for blame:

- You are a stupid idiot.
- It is your fault.
- Can't you do anything right?
- Because I said so.
- You don't know.
- You are flawed.
- If it weren't for you this would be a success.
- I am right and you are wrong.
- You are doing it wrong.
- You are a failure.
- What you think is inconsequential and doesn't make a difference.

- "The only problem with ____ is that he just doesn't step up."
- "This is not my problem."
- "I don't know what you are complaining about."
- "I already heard that feedback and it is not valid."
- "Do you think you can move ANY slower?"
- "How many times do I have to tell you?"

YOU ARE IN ADVERSARY WHEN:

1. You are always irritated at other people's short-comings and think about how other people should change.

2. You say, "Yes, but..." a lot.

3. You rarely step into the other people's shoes to see their side of things.

4. You see yourself as doing it right while everyone else is doing it wrong.

5. You are quick to blame others.

"Anger is the wind which blows out the lamp of the mind."
—Robert Green Ingersoll

STRATEGIES TO NEUTRALIZE YOUR ADVERSARIAL WAY OF THINKING

1. Realize that your attitude is creating the biggest part of the problem.

2. Step into the others' shoes and feel how your negativity impacts them.

3. Realize that you stay on the offensive so that others will not see your faults.

4. Let other people be right.

5. Realize that you are blocking the best solution from coming forward.

6. It is not up to others to step up; it is up to you to create a safe space.

7. Realize where you are not trusting people.

8. Accept that you are choosing being right over the choosing what is true.

9. Admit that you are not open minded.

10. Remind yourself of your goals and how you can support others to get there.

11. Think of the positives and mention them.

12. Identify what you are afraid might happen.

13. Identify where you feel helpless.

14. Ask yourself how what is happening is your responsibility.

15. What do you want for yourself? for others?

16. Where do you blame others rather than taking responsibility?

17. Make fun of yourself.

18. Notice where you use sarcasm rather than offering a constructive comment

19. Realize that your anger is moving against a constructive goal.

20. Acknowledge people twice as much as you criticize them.

21. Question how your negativity can lead to a positive result.

22. "Never go to bed mad. Stay up and fight."
    —Phyllis Diller

23. "Always write angry letters to your enemies. Never mail them."
    —James Fallows

24. "Get mad, then get over it." —Colin Powell

25. "Always forgive your enemies—nothing annoys them so much." —Oscar Wilde

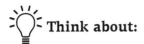 **Think about:**

1. What situations or people trigger you into acting in the Adversary mode?

2. What do you say to yourself when you are in the Adversary mode?

3. Describe the role of the Adversary to someone you are close to. Ask that person to point out to you when you exhibit adversarial behaviors.

4. Which of the Adversary Neutralizers work the best for you? Notice how you "feel" internally once you have neutralized that state.

5. Write the neutralizers that work the best for you. Practice, practice, practice implementing them.

6. What other elements might you substitute for the Adversary that fit for your experience? What negative emotions and attributes are related to your personal Adversarial elements?

"For every minute you remain angry,
you give up sixty seconds of peace of mind."
—Ralph Waldo Emerson

RESCUER—
THE DARK SIDE OF ALTRUISM

"Intolerance is the most socially acceptable form of egotism,
for it permits us to assume superiority
without personal boasting."
—Sydney J. Harris

Rescuers put people down and elevate themselves by creating situations where they are needed but do nothing to improve others.

The Proud Rescuer

Martha had an ingenious way of inserting herself into other people's projects. She would first swoop by and point out what was missing. She made sure she was the one who could fix the problem but when invited to make her contribution, rather than participate, she would continue to point out more problems. Basically, she spent her time expanding her scope of potential intervention. Pretty soon, she was taking over many aspects of the project, while, in her mind, she was belittling the people involved by saying to herself, "It's a good thing that I am here to fix this." When the project was finished, she took pride in telling everyone how she saved the day.

Rescuers just want to "help," but underneath their seeming kindness is an active subtext that says, "I am helping you because you don't have what it takes and I do." The Rescuer holds a judgment of others as being inadequate and incapable. As a Rescuer, you perceive what is missing and put yourself in a superior role that minimizes the other person's power, effectiveness, skills, and talents. Unlike the Adversary, who will sit on the sidelines and criticize, the Rescuer will not hesitate to jump right on to the playing field, take over, and take all the credit. Rescuers will never confront a person in an honest way to express their true needs. That is because inside they are afraid that they are truly weak, and so prefer to maintain the bravado of superiority.

At home Martha took over her kids' homework. She did it for them without explaining what she did or how she solved the problems. Her kids were left without a clue as to what to do. Her friends noticed that she would "help" them out but really just took over, pushing them out of the way with a nice smile on her face. Her friends were always baffled at how she seemed to take control in such a nice way. One day one of her friends said she was going to bake some cookies for her son's class and Martha's instant response was, "Oh, I'll bake them for you."

The Rescuer sees the world as a place that needs their salvation. The Rescuer's point of view has the one-upmanship of the Adversary and the artificial niceness of the Victim. Rescuers are on the hunt for what is missing, but only if what is missing is what they have to offer. The Rescuer elevates themselves in the presence of the Victim and validates the Victim's thought that she is helpless and the situation is hopeless for her.

The Rescuer says, "Yes, you are helpless and hopeless and I can take care of it. I have the courage. I have the skills. I have whatever is needed to make the situation right." The Rescuer lives in an altruistic critical mode of superiority: "I'll save the day. I'll do my heroics and when it comes time for credit I will take the credit."

Rescuers can look like team players, but they are not. A team player is somebody who comes in and does what needs to be done. He does it and then he disappears after it is done, not expecting to take credit for his effort. The Rescuer comes in, does what needs to be done, expecting the credit in fact to kind of puff himself up. Basically a Rescuer will give you a false sense of hope because you feel relieved that he is taking care of things and freeing you from your responsibilities. In the case of the Victim it is like, "Oh good, somebody here is powerful, can do it and can take care of it." But the true Rescuer will never empower a Victim because that would eliminate the Rescuer's need to be needed.

HOW YOU THINK WHEN YOU ARE IN RESCUER:

- You are just not cutting it; I can.
- I have what is needed.
- No one recognizes my importance.
- Everything will fall apart if I go away.
- There is no one to replace me.
- I resent taking on your work, but you will never know it
- You will never meet expectations.
- I always have to fill in for you.
- You will crumble if I confront you with your problems
- I am doing a job of two or three people but only get paid for one.
- No one else will do it if I don't.

YOU ARE IN RESCUER WHEN:

1. You take over rather than teach.

2. You see yourself as the only one who is capable.

3. You listen to people complain about the same things over and over.

4. When the job is done you want the credit.

5. You think the project, work, business would fall apart if you were not there because you think you are responsible for everything.

STRATEGIES TO NEUTRALIZE YOUR RESCUER WAY OF THINKING:

1. Create situations where you teach rather than take over

2. Own your criticism of others—look for where you can coach them constructively.

3. When a person repeats the same old story again, stop them and ask, "What do you want in this situation? What are you going to do to move in that direction?"

4. If you take on a task for someone, set up a time to teach the person how to do the task.

5. When you help someone out, let go of any expectation to be acknowledged for helping.

6. Stop from automatically volunteering your time. Ask yourself if you really have the time or energy to freely take on the task.

7. When a person tells the same old story again stop the person and say, "I notice that this situation seems to keep reoccurring for you. What is your role in perpetuating the problem?"

8. Realize that selfless service is different from rescuing.

9. Let people know where they need to improve.

10. Understand that letting people struggle with a problem can be a great learning opportunity for them.

11. Don't rob people of the opportunity to learn something you have already mastered.

12. Work to train people so they can be better than you.

13. Look for people who can take over your job.

14. Teach people to do what you do.

15. Make yourself dispensable by teaching others.

16. Realize that the true spirit of giving is without expectation for return.

"Strive not to be a success, but rather to be of value."
—Albert Einstein

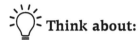 **Think about:**

1. What situations or people trigger you into the Rescuer mode?

2. What do you say to yourself when you are in the Rescuer mode?

3. Describe the Rescuer mode to a close friend. Ask her to recall times when she saw you in that mode.

4. Go teach the skill to a person that you have been Rescuing.

5. Which of the Rescuer Neutralizers work the best for you? Write them down. What other elements might you substitute for the Rescuer that fit for your experience? What negative emotions and attributes are related to your personal Rescuer elements?

17. THE POSITIVE INTENT MOLECULE

"I've missed more than 9,000 shots in my career. I've lost almost 300 games. Twenty-six times, I've been trusted to take the game-winning shot and missed. I've failed over and over and over again in my life. And that is why I succeed."
—Michael Jordan

Building positive intent and creating constructive loops and patterns are easy. Instead of playing the Victim, Adversary, or Rescuer, you have new options to strengthen your talents and positive gifts. You can now become a Visionary, Activator, and Coach. But once you learn to assume these roles you will need diligent commitment and practice to make them a part of your automatic responses and part of your nervous system. You will also need to recognize the interrelationship between those three crucial roles to determine how to strengthen them further. This is all about building leadership and promoting action and intention from a positive frame of mind and awareness.

Fred was going through an intense weight training program. One day his coach had a halting look on his face, stopped the workout, and said, "Well, you are getting stronger than I am."

Fred looked at him, puzzled, and said, "That's the whole purpose, to make me strong."

The trainer said, "But you are the first person I have coached who has gotten stronger than me."

Fred then explained, "When I teach somebody to become a public speaker I give them all of my secrets, hopefully to make them better than I am. Through their success, I will learn something that will make me better. I am not afraid of somebody outshining me. I intentionally want to develop people around me who surpass me." That is the attitude that successful leaders take. Leaders are about developing leaders.

Fred gave his coach some coaching on how to be a trainer who operates from Positive Intention. As you engage in building your Positive Intent Molecule, you'll focus on your current vision and goals, what actions you will take to get there, and how to support and develop the people around you.

"I am enough of an artist to draw freely upon my imagination."
—Albert Einstein

VISIONARY

What does it mean to be a Visionary? As a Visionary you step outside of the conventions of today into a much larger way of thinking and imagining. Unfettered by the constraints of the past, not fazed by shoulds and have to's, a Visionary is bold and goes beyond "what is" into "what can and will be." A Visionary refuses to be bound by the laws and rules of today because she pulls the future into the moment. Of course, it isn't always easy. That's because a Visionary often needs to commit to a vision that has no tangible evidence...yet. This is a risky position, but the Visionary intuits, knows, and is confident in what is to be. Visionaries respect their vision and help it become manifest and real because they are willing to see it, feel it, speak it, and bring it into being. It truly is making something out of nothing. A Visionary lives in a state of commitment

151

to what is to become and is always engaged in bringing something new into this world, be it a new idea, a product, or an entire reality. As a Visionary you don't just talk about the future, it is as if you are the vision of tomorrow speaking itself into existence today.

Sherry has a natural ability to imagine what the world will look like in ten years. She doesn't force herself because her mind simply goes into Visionary mode. When listening to a business presentation, she naturally thinks about long-term implications. She often asks questions that make people think outside of the box. When she presents ideas she always begins by painting a picture of how the business will look in the future. People are always captivated by her talks because she brings her vision to life.

(The book *Daring to Have the Real Conversation in Business* covers the best practices about presenting your vision to your organization.)

The Visionary's job is to communicate the future happening now, happening today, embodying it into the present moment and making it a real tangible experience. A Visionary is not just the idea maker. The work is not done until the vision is fully realized.

When Sherry was buying a house, she always saw how the house would look once she had made it the way she wanted. She amazed her friends at the transformations that her homes went through as she worked on them. To Sherry it was very natural to see the possible future in what was happening today.

Visionaries bring a sense of inspiration because they build a window into the future that is palpable, filled with passion and excitement for what is to become.

Visionary Cycle

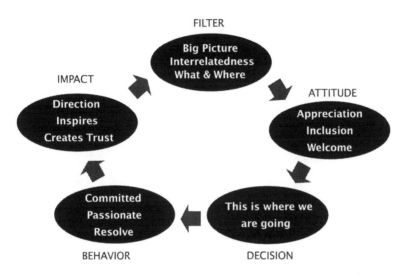

"*Visionary people face the same problems everyone else faces; but rather than get paralyzed by their problems, visionaries immediately commit themselves to finding a solution.*"
—Bill Hybels

WHAT MAKES A VISIONARY TICK

Visionaries exist at the 50,000-foot level. They see the big picture, 360 degrees around. They are also focused on the course and direction, the tangible questions such as the "what is going to be accomplished," "where are we going" issues. From their huge vantage point, Visionaries see the interrelatedness of things. As a Visionary, your mind is occupied with the future, and what will be. You have a visceral feeling about the vision. It registers in the core of your body as a deep sense of confidence. The vision has a three-dimensional quality to it that makes it very real. You feel the outreaching possibilities of the vision and how this vision interconnects with other people, systems, and organizations.

Visionaries exude an appreciation for what is around them. Since Visionaries see the interconnection of all, they can recognize the value in each person, each component, and their attitude is one of inclusion. Visionaries create an environment everyone wants to inhabit. It is seductive to be part of their big picture. This is not by accident. They know how to engage and invite all the different elements and personalities into the whole so that they can interact in a productive way.

Visionaries know that new courses and directions bring challenges as well. When those problems arise the Visionary keeps focused on the goal. The Visionary doesn't live in denial, acknowledges the obstacle, and will often think about how that problem could be solved differently in the future state of the vision.

The Visionary consistently reminds us of where we are going. They always keep us focused on the direction. As a Visionary you are naturally very passionate. People feel your deep commitment and resolve to reach the goal. Because you are congruent in your speech and action you instill trust in those around you. You are living and breathing that future vision. They look to your commitment and leadership in times of challenge and stress.

YOU ARE IN VISIONARY WHEN:

1. You have a clear vision for the future.

2. You are able to communicate your vision to others in a way that energizes and motivates.

3. You see how things are interrelated.

4. You are committed to the vision.

5. In the face of challenges, you keep the focus of others and yourself on the goal.

STRATEGIES FOR ENHANCING YOUR VISIONARY QUALITIES

To enhance your ability to be a Visionary you need to be a forward thinker. You need to look into the future and ask, "What is the goal that I want to accomplish? What will it look like when it is accomplished? What will people be saying? What will it feel like?"

- Create a rich description of the future, one that you can describe from multiple perspectives.

- Think about stepping into the shoes of the person or people you will be talking to.

- Tailor your communication so that it will resonate with what is important to them. Describe what will happen when the vision is accomplished. What is the actual result? What would be the impact on people, on systems, on the environment, on organizations? Who will be affected by this vision? Who is included? Who is not included?

You need a very clear idea of the inner connections with and implications of entities that are outside of the direct goal itself. Your description should include what is going to be different. Include what the challenges are going to be to get there. No worthwhile goal is easily accomplished without having to overcome challenges.

- Take some time to think about what those impacts might be. What are some of the other benefits? What's the qualitative change that will take place? How would the quality of people's lives, their experience, their work experience, their play experience, their family experience be changed?

- Look for what is not obvious. Look for different angles. Think of metaphors that you can use to describe the change.

- Lastly, and probably most importantly, what is in it for other people? "Why should I get involved?" needs to be answered. Why should I put my time and energy into this vision and into this goal? You want to make it something that brings you to life, that fills you with energy and vibrancy as you talk about it and have a clear understanding of your constituency and how it will impact and benefit them as well.

StrengthsFinder[3] Themes of Visionary

The following list includes ways that you can strengthen your Visionary qualities:

- **Analytical**—Search for the reasons and underlying causes. Increase your ability to think about all the factors that might affect a situation.

- **Belief**—Recognize your core values that are unchanging and serve as the foundation for your purpose in life.

- **Command**—Be fully present. Take control of a situation and make the needed decisions.

- **Connectedness**—See the links between all things. Realize that there are few coincidences and that events usually have an underlying reason.

- **Context**—Take into account the past and understand the timeline and sequence of how the present state came into existence.

- **Futuristic**—Live and be inspired by the future and what could be. Communicate your vision of the future

- **Harmony**—Look for areas where there is a natural overlap of agreement. Seek to create alignment where agreement is not possible.

- **Ideation**—Enjoy when the light bulb pops on and you are filled with new ideas. Create that environment for others.

- **Includer**—Remember to engage those who are on the fringe. Bring in their ideas and perspectives

- **Input**—Appreciate your thirst to know more. Value your collections of knowledge and experience.

- **Intellection**—Be introspective and also engage in thoughtful discussion with others.

- **Positivity**—Cultivate contagious enthusiasm. Your upbeat attitude ignites passion in others

- **Woo**—Break the ice and win people over with positivity and possibility. Enjoy connecting with others.

"If we knew what it was we were doing,
it would not be called research, would it?"
—Albert Einstein

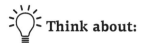 **Think about:**

1. Who are visionaries that have inspired you? What was it about them that you found so inspiring?

2. In the above example, how would you create that type of impact on others?

3. Explain one of your visions to a friend. Notice their nonverbal response and ask, "Are you inspired or energized by what I said?"

4. Ask your friend to coach you on how to make your vision more compelling

5. What would you like to bring into the world that would be of service to others?

6. What other elements or qualities might you substitute for the Visionary to make it personal and fitting for you? What positive emotions and attributes are related to your personal Visionary elements?

> *"Success isn't a result of spontaneous combustion.*
> *You must set yourself on fire."*
> **—Arnold H. Glasow**

ACTIVATOR

Activators are the catalysts. Catalysts increase the rate of a reaction. A Catalyst is not consumed by the reaction itself. Activators/Catalysts that speed the reaction are called positive Activators. Activators favorably affect their environment, and they can be transformative energizers for individuals, groups, and projects. The Activator works between where we are today and the vision of tomorrow. They create the steps that bridge today to the vision of to-morrow. An Activator answers the question, "How are we going to get there?" The Activator is very pragmatic and concrete. They are great architects of process, identifying roles and responsibilities, milestones and action timelines. This is one of the mechanisms that allow Activators to get things to happen. Activators are good at communicating and describing how you will achieve the goals. Activators provide people with what needs to be done next. The Activator brings forth a sense of urgency, yet he still has one foot firmly in the reality of today to pull it forward, providing the pathway, the steps, to strategize and be the communicator to bring people forward.

Sharon is a great project manager. The minute she hears someone share a big idea, her mind immediately thinks about the timelines and deliverables, roles and responsibilities, what it will take to get there. By the time she walks out of the room she has a good idea of how to get the vision to manifest. She sets up meetings with her project teams and explains the goals and her high level timeline, then has her team break out into smaller groups to flesh out the work plans. She knows that by having regular communication she will be more successful in executing the plan, so she always insists that the team set up a communication schedule with each work plan.

When Sharon and her family decided to go on vacation, Sharon created the schedule for the entire trip and even for the preparation. She was very upbeat and excited and created a great deal of enthusiasm for her family. Everyone knew what was going to happen and what they needed to do to get ready.

Activators say, "Hey, come on, let's go. We don't have all day. We must start taking action immediately. This is your first step. This is the next step." The Activator paves the way to the vision. Activators get traction and initiate or accelerate movement. They are very logical. They are very literal. They think in tangible terms, and because they can see the vision, they provide the actual steps to deal with the challenges, to deal with the blockages, to deal with the things that might get in the way of manifesting the vision. The Visionary knows that there are going to be challenges and obstacles to getting to the goal. The Activator plots the actual course to the vision and this activity creates confidence and strength, two qualities of the Positive Intent Molecule.

The Activator Cycle

"A positive attitude causes a chain reaction
of positive thoughts, events and outcomes.
It is a catalyst and it sparks extraordinary results."
—Wade Boggs

The Visionary points to the goal, the "what" and the "where." The Activator brings forward the "how" we are going to get there that fosters the can-do attitude. The Activator sees the ways around and through obstacles and brings them to resolution so the result is realized.

162

YOU ARE AN ACTIVATOR WHEN:

1. You love organizing and getting people moving toward the goal

2. You live by your timelines

3. You are accountable and hold people accountable in a way that motivates them to do their best.

4. You get results.

5. You don't mind rocking the boat to get things moving.

STRATEGIES FOR ENHANCING YOUR ACTIVATOR QUALITIES

An Activator is always working toward the goal. The Activator has a thorough understanding of the present state, where people are today, and what the condition of systems thinking, emotions, and morale is. Where are people coming from? What is their thinking around the goal? Are they clear about what it is? Do they need to be educated? Do they need some instructions or guidance, and if so, what is the best method to deliver that so that they can completely, in a sense, own the goal for themselves? What is the goal? The Activator always makes sure that the goal has been clearly identified and crystallized, and then they plot the course.

"In a gentle way, you can shake the world."
—Mohandas Gandhi

StrengthsFinder[4] Characteristics of the Activator

- **Achiever**—Appreciate your stamina and hard work. Notice how much satisfaction you get from being busy and productive.

- **Activator**—Turn thoughts into action. Realize your impatience can be transformed into urgency.

- **Competition**—Enjoy your competitive nature. Create opportunities for healthy competition. Keep your sense of humor and teamwork. Remember to honor the competition for bringing out the best in you.

- **Deliberative**—Be rigorous in making decisions or choices. Anticipate the obstacles and plan for them.

- **Focus**—Stay on track and follow through. When the unexpected arises make the corrections necessary to prioritize and navigate back on course.

- **Responsibility**—Follow through on your word. Be an owner of the goal and the process to get there. When setbacks occur, communicate to those who are waiting on you so they can adjust their expectations. No excuses.

- **Restorative**—Tap your ability to figure out what is wrong and resolve it. Deal with problems proactively.

---

[4] Now Discover Your Strengths, Marcus Buckingham StrengthsFinder 2000, 2006-2009 Gallup, Inc. www. strengths.gallup.com

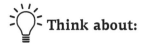 **Think about:**

1. Think of three people who are great Activators. How did they impact you and others?

2. How would you create that type of impact on others?

3. Take a simple goal that you have. Write out your specific work plan to accomplish your goal. Detail what activities will happen at what specific time.

4. Review your plan with a close friend. Ask her to check in with you at specific times to see how you are doing with your plan.

5. What two areas in your life could use a sense of urgency to get things done?

6. What other elements might you substitute for the Activator to make it personal and fitting for you? What positive emotions and attributes are related to your personal Activator elements?.

"When it is obvious that the goals cannot be reached,
don't adjust the goals, adjust the action steps."
—Confucius

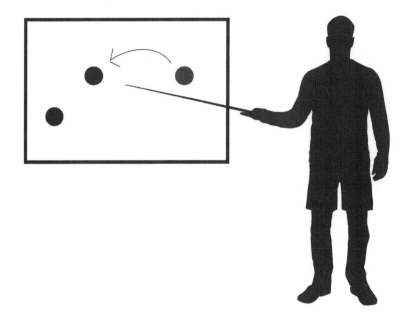

COACH

"Every block of stone has a statue inside it and it is the task of the sculptor to discover it."
—Michelangelo

The Visionary creates the vision, the Activator plots the course to get there, and the Coach is there beside you to encourage you to be your best as you work toward the goals. Coaches help people become capable and confident. Coaches see you in a unique way. They see your inner strengths, potential, and capabilities. A Coach creates the environment and stimulation so you can be your best and really shine.

The Coach sees you as a talented and capable person. The Coach speaks to your magnificence and holds a high standard of performance. The Coach's belief in you motivates you to stretch beyond your normal bounds and do incredible things. Coaches help you have breakthroughs to discover your inner talent.

The Coach balances patience with high expectations and is firm in encouraging you to go beyond what you thought was possible. In the same way the Activator bridges the present and the vision, the Coach sees where you are today and helps you connect the dots to reach your full potential. The Coach speaks to your full capability and creates the opportunity for you to uncover and claim more of your power.

Coaches interact with you in a very systematic way to bring forth your strengths and capabilities. They facilitate results by supporting your achievement and development. A Coach is not easy on you and yet despite their demanding nature, coaches are compassionate. A Coach brings forth your best without being harsh or disrespectful. Coaches help you grow and develop and go beyond your fears and doubts. A Coach shows you how to step outside of yourself and to allow new things in. A Coach is committed to creating the environment for you to grow in a very natural and organic way that maximizes your talents.

Barry has a natural way of asking great questions when people come to him with problems about their work. He knows that is much more powerful to stimulate a person's thinking than just to tell them the answer. He would ask,

"Have you thought about it this way....?", "What would happen if you considered...?" He asked questions that would lead the person to discover the answer for himself, yet his questions were very focused and intentional. People would always feel great after meeting with him because they would learn something.

A Coach does not force you into anything. Coaches create the environment and support for you to unfold in a very natural and personally ecological (personal ecology—what will work for the person) way. A Coach doesn't use force because force is not really necessary in coaching. A Coach provides the tools for development, and while this process may have it is moments of discomfort, embarrassment, and hard work, a Coach does not shy away because a Coach believes that you are able to metabolize your own inner strength and knows that you will naturally grow.

When Barry's kids had problems with their homework he would ask them questions that would let them discover how to solve the problems without having to tell them exactly what to do. A Coach operates from positive intent. They see that in us and interact with us to bring forth positive intent in our thinking action and words.

Coach

"*Always keep an open mind and a compassionate heart.*"
—Phil Jackson

STRATEGIES FOR ENHANCING YOUR INNER COACH

The Coach is focused on the people element, the "who." For each person, identify what their strengths and talents are and look at the organization of people and their strengths and talents against the goals that need to be met. Do they have the right combination of people there? If there are gaps in the talent that is needed, do you want to bring in new talent or do you want to train the existing talent that you have?

Keep in mind that when you are developing people, you want to develop them along the axis of their strengths, not try to make up for their weaknesses. Though in the larger sense you are looking at the overall goal, look at the talent pool that you have and do an assessment. Determine each individual's strengths and abilities and determine how you can interact with them to bring forward their strengths and abilities.

The simple coaching process can look like this. There is a goal. Do you understand it? What do you have? What talents to you have and what capabilities do you have to reach that goal? What is it that you need? How can you go about getting what you need to get there? When will all of this take place? What can I do to support you getting what you need to accomplish the goal?

StrengthsFinder³ Themes for strengthening for the Coach

- **Consistency**—Ensure that people are treated the same. Set up clear rules and adhere to them. Eliminate favorites.

- **Developer**—Recognize and cultivate the innate talent and capability in others. Notice and reward incremental improvements.

- **Discipline**—Create an ordered world and healthy routines to follow. Be a role model and hold others to the discipline that will improve them.

- **Empathy**—Put yourself in the shoes of other people and feel and think as they do. Maintain this awareness in your interactions with others.

- **Individualization**—Appreciate and cultivate the unique qualities of each person. Look to see how diversity can be brought into harmony in situations.

- **Learner** –- Cultivate your desire to learn and continuously improve. Notice how much you enjoy the process of learning something for the sake of learning.

- **Maximizer**—Engage a person's/group's strengths to create excellence. Take what is good and make it great.

- **Self-Assurance**—Own your confidence in your ability to manage your life. Use your inner guidance to make your life's decisions.

- **Significance**—Realize that your reputation is critical in your ability to influence and lead others. Strategically manage your reputation to achieve goals.

- **Relator**—Enjoy the deep satisfaction you derive from working hard with friends to achieve a goal.

"Courage is being scared to death... and saddling up anyway."
—John Wayne

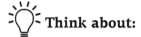 **Think about:**

1. List some great coaches.

2. What do they do that creates results? How can you do that in your life?

3. Ask a friend to coach you on a goal that you have.

4. What are 3—5 coaching questions they can ask you to help keep you on track? At what interval do you want them to coach you?

5. What are a couple of areas you could be coached in? Who could you coach?

6. What other elements might you substitute for the Coach to make it personal and fitting for you? What positive emotions and attributes are related to your personal Coach elements?

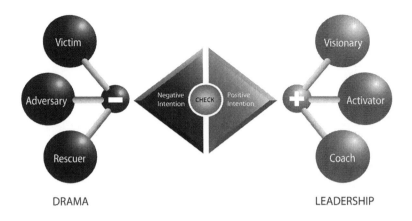

DRAMA   LEADERSHIP

BIRD'S EYE VIEW

"Never confuse motion with action."
—Benjamin Franklin

Let's now take the observer's view of the two classic molecules. When you assume Negative Intention you will be in the Negative Intent Molecule and take on the attitudes of the Victim, Adversary, and Rescuer. To review, the Victim assumes negative intent by creating negative thoughts about him- or herself and about the world that she imagines is going to take advantage of, punish, or hurt. The Adversary assumes negative by being right and making others wrong. The Rescuer assumes negative intent, by seeing the world as a helpless place needing his help and salvation. The three points on the Negative Intent Molecule represent a self-perpetuating, vicious cycle and each of these points is a support for the other two. The Victim needs an Adversary to project his power on to and to maintain their sense of helplessness. The Adversary needs a Victim as the basis for her self confidence. The Rescuer needs a Victim and an Adversary to maintain his sense of superiority.

In the Positive Intent Molecule you can see that the Visionary keeps the focus on the goals, the results, and where you are going to be. The Activator is focused on the process to get to the goal, roles and responsibilities, and sustaining a sense of urgency and accountability to reach the goals. The Coach focuses on developing and supporting people.

You can see the relationship and the interdependency of the three different points in the Positive Intent Molecule. You need all three to have full and robust leadership based on Positive Intention. If you have an Activator without a Visionary you have chaos. People will be scrambling around with a sense of urgency but not really knowing where they are going. If you have an Activator without the Coach you have kind of a mechanistic heartless organization that doesn't really care about its people. If you have a Visionary without an Activator you have pie in the sky, and a Visionary without a Coach is all alone. A Coach without a Visionary could be a real tyrant and a Coach without an Activator really doesn't have a specific purpose or pathway.

If we were to relate the Positive Intention molecule to the body, the Visionary is the head, the Activator is the legs, and the coach is the heart. The Visionary represents the idea, the Activator is action, and Coach represents the passion.

Practice looking at your mind and personality from this point of neutrality and you will create a good place to make intentional changes in how you think.

The Molecules Matrix is a chart that gives you the detail about the perceptual-behavioral cycles for each point. The Molecules Matrix allows you to dial into where you are operating from.

1. The FILTERS that you perceive the world through. What you notice.

2. The ATTITUDE and feeling tone for each point.

3. The DECISION for how that point views and solves problems.

4. The BEHAVIORS expressed for each point.

5. The IMPACT that you have on others.

Check Your Attitude Matrix

PERCEPTUAL LOOP	NEGATIVE INTENTION			POSITIVE INTENTION		
	VICTIM	ADVERSARY	RESCUER	VISIONARY	ACTIVATOR	COACH
FILTER	Powerless Threatened Betrayal	What's Wrong Criticism Fault Finding	What's Missing Weaknesses	Big Picture Interrelatedness What	Steps Challenges How	Talents Strength Who
ATTITUDE	Inferiority At Fault Resigned	Condescending Arrogant Outrage	Minimizes Better Than You Superiority	Appreciation Inclusion	Can Do Urgency Focus	Maximizes Others
DECISION	It's hopeless I'm helpless	I'm Right You're Wrong	I will save you You can't help yourself	This is where we are going	Let's make it happen	You have got what it takes
BEHAVIOR	Passive-Aggressive Excuses	Attack Blame Defensive	Rescues Takes Over Hijacks Credit	Committed Passionate Resolve	Accountable Strategizes Communicates	Guidance Empowers Motivates
IMPACT	Energy Drain Frustration Sabotage	Make Wrong Pressure Hostility	Disempowers False Hope No Growth	Direction Inspires Creates Trust	Engagement Acceleration Action	Confidence Results

18. MAKE YOUR MOLECULES

You've had the opportunity to read about the classic positive and negative intention molecules. They are examples of the essential elements for leadership and drama. You have a unique way that you create positive and negative molecules. The idea is to use the classic positive and negative molecules to further develop your awareness and learning. Your job now is to create your own positive and negative intention molecules. Think about the three areas of your life, work, home and relationships and for each of those situations think about the key three positive elements and the three key negative elements as they relate to you personally. Below are some examples so that you can see how that could work. Take some time to sketch out, play around with developing your own model of molecules that works for you that you can personally relate to very easily and directly. Once you have that, then it'll be much easier for you to recognize when you're in positive intention and negative intention and what to do when you're in negative intention to switch to positive. Remember—the three key elements are in the circles and the interconnecting lines indicate the sub elements that work to interconnect the elements and hold this structure in place.

Positive Intention Molecules

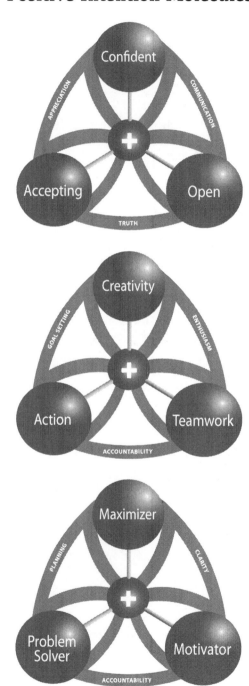

Negative Intention Molecules

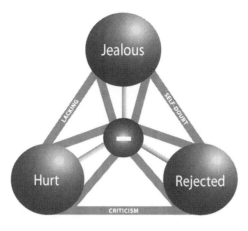

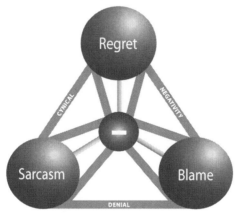

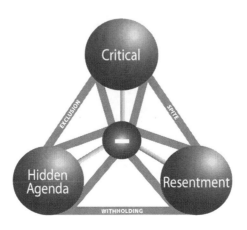

Your Personal Molecules

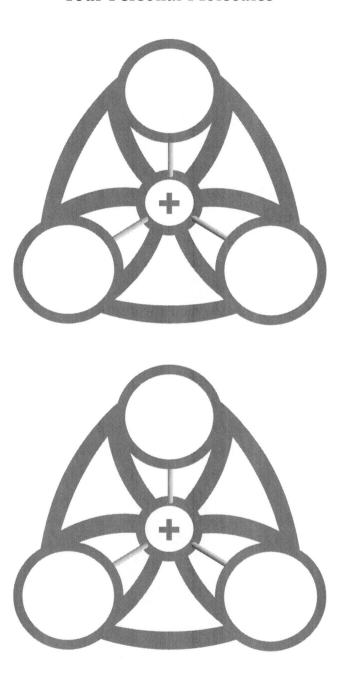

IV
Check Your Attitude

"Without change, something sleeps inside us, and seldom awakens. The sleeper must awaken."
—Frank Herbert

What To Do When You Get To The Door

When you feel healthy it is hardly the time you think about going to see the doctor. Likewise, when you are doing well and things are working in your life, you are probably not thinking about how to get out of negative thoughts or feelings. Typically it is not until you are stuck or feeling lousy that you think about doing something about it. It's really a good idea to think about your awareness, attitude, and action before things go south. Athletes don't wait until they feel weak to practice; they practice all along to make themselves stronger. A daily focus and practice is the best way to make progress. One of the easiest ways is to keep the awareness alive is by talking about your process with friends, family, and work colleagues. In this way you will widen your support network and create a learning opportunity as well as a vital support network. People learn best by hearing each other's stories. As you talk about your perceptions and process, others will learn from your examples.

This section covers:

1. What to do when you find yourself getting sucked into the Negative Intent Molecule; how to handle situations when your energy feels like it is dragging you downward into a negative spiral.

2. How to focus your life around your core values.

3. Discovering your personal purpose in life as a guiding principle.

First we will focus on how to turn things around when you are in a negative place. The second chapter is about your core values and how you can use them to enhance your life. The third chapter is about your purpose in life. Your purpose creates a focus to encourage you to give your gifts to the world throughout your life. As your life evolves you will revisit these three practices to sustain your growth and development.

"Once you replace negative thoughts with positive ones, you'll start having positive results."
—Willie Nelson

19. ACTION

"Do you want to know who you are? Don't ask. Act!
Action will delineate and define you."
—Thomas Jefferson

Your actions create an environment around you, that can be called your personal culture. If you have an attitude of positive intent, it will stimulate an environment of positive intent around you. That is what you will perceive and what people will experience when they are in your presence. If you have an attitude of negative intent, then you will experience negativity around you. You will not be open to what is going on and people around you will have a similar experience as well. If you think about many of the great leaders in our time, when things got difficult they kept a positive attitude. This is what actually led people to a successful outcome even when the external circumstances seemed to be dire. Likewise, by having a Positive Intention in your attitude you will be able to create success as you navigate your way through your life.

Not only are actions what you see out there in the world, but there is also a huge battery of micro or subtle actions that includes your expressions, nonverbal cues, the tone of your voice, your body posture, and all the things that you express while you communicate. So action is not only obvious but also very subtle, and the subtleties can be significant.

Think of what someone would notice from an observer's point of view. This kind of witnessing requires a much greater level of awareness than just checking off a list of behaviors of things that you should or shouldn't do. Since your micro behaviors, like the tone of your voice, reflect your attitudes, it is crucial to build on your awareness. As you become more and more aware you will discover you can scope out a lot about what you are thinking. In turn, you'll find how what you think affects how you express yourself, and in turn, how you are perceived. Your attitude about the variety of situations you encounter all day long dictates and defines your actions from the micro to the macro level.

It is essential to build awareness and a positive attitude; real transformation happens when you make changes in your attitude and behaviors/tangible actions. Your actions are the result of your awareness, your attitude (mental and emotional processes). To intentionally create positive action, follow these steps:

1. Be aware of your thinking, attitudes, and actions.

2. Become aware of what triggers you into a negative frame of mind.

3. Pause to change the fundamental intention of your thinking from negative to Positive Intention. Notice what your choices are.

4. Generate a positive behavior and impact that is in alignment with your Positive Intention.

5. Once you act, check to verify the actual impact of your action.

"People don't resist change. They resist being changed!"
—Peter Senge

Choice Point

"One's action ought to come out of an achieved stillness:
not to be mere rushing on."
—D.H. Lawrence

You come to the stop sign and stop, put your car in neutral, and take a breath. You are at the Choice Point. Choice point means you are poised and ready to choose. You are at a place mentally where you are not trying to move in any particular direction and your are not resisting or avoiding anything. Your emotions are in neutral as well. You are mentally and emotionally in the neutral gear.

Choice point is like your breathing. There is a point in between when your inhale ends and your exhale begins—that is the choice point. Choice point is also like the moment in between trapezes for the trapeze artist. You have let go of the past and get to choose what happens next. There is a quality of freedom in that moment. You are not trying to resist something bad from the past happening "again." You are not forcing something to happen in the future either.

When you are at a Choice Point you are able to freely choose.

GETTING INTO THE CHOICE POINT ZONE

There are a few tips that will help you get into your Choice Point zone.

1. Close your door, turn off the ringer and vibrator on your phone, and turn off the computer monitor.

2. Relax your muscles. Tension is a sign you are resisting or are stressed. Take a few minutes to relax physically. Do some stretching or try self massage on your neck and shoulders.

3. Take a few deep breaths. Count from backwards from ten to one slowly, with one count for each breath. Chill out.

It may seem like a long time, but in reality it only takes about three minutes to bring yourself to a calm, relaxed state. Now you are ready to choose.

WHAT KEEPS YOU OUT OF THE CHOICE POINT ZONE?

You actually talk yourself out of the choice point zone. Your words and language are powerful. If you say, "I can't do math," "I can't read fast," "It's impossible to make a million dollars honestly," you have eliminated those choices as possibilities. We often interpret them as absolute statements and not something that can be changed. If we say that we can't do something or that something is impossible, chances are it is just a belief about ourselves. In NeuroLinguistic Programming (NLP) these language phrases that we say to ourselves that limit possibilities are called modal operators of possibility and necessity. These examples show limitations that are based on belief—not objective fact.

When you use the words "can't" or "impossible" you set up an outcome and then put it out of reach. When you use the words "should," "should not," "must," "must not," "ought," or "ought not," you are also limiting yourself. For example, "I have to balance my check book after every check," or "I should not eat too much meat."

NLP provides several tools to free up your thinking to get to the Choice Point zone. Ask yourself, "What

would happen if I did?" or "What stops me?" or "How do I stop myself?" If you want to drill down further, ask:

- Do I have a good understanding of what the goal, or outcome, is?

- Do I understand why I want it?

- Why do I think I can't achieve it?

- What are the consequences if I do achieve it?

- What can I do to get it?

Once the consequences and barriers have been explored, further examination may show the goal to be less challenging than originally thought and you will be able to enter the Choice Point zone.

In order to get closer to the choice point, replace "I can't" with "I won't" or "I am choosing not to." This makes it is a choice and not an absolute fact. For example, when you change "I can't give a speech in front of a thousand people" to "I am choosing not to give a speech in front of a thousand people," it puts you in the driver's seat. You are making it a conscious choice—giving a speech in front of a thousand people is a difficult task, but it isn't impossible.

"If you limit your choices only to what seems possible or reasonable, you disconnect yourself from what you truly want, and all that is left is compromise."
—Robert Fritz

20. CHECKING YOUR ATTITUDE

"If you don't like something, change it.
If you can't change it, change your attitude."
—**Maya Angelou**

HOW TO GET OUT OF THE NEGATIVE INTENT MOLECULE

This chapter tells you what to do when you find yourself getting sucked into the Negative Intent Molecule, when your energy feels like it is dragging you down and you are in that downward spiral. In the simplest of terms, Checking Your Attitude at the Door is about giving people and yourself the benefit of the doubt. This entails pausing for a moment when something happens that normally would upset you, reflecting on what is happening in your mind, and then choosing a positive attitude to replace your negative thinking. The process of Checking Your Attitude requires that you create an observer's state of mind. This means that you are able to watch your mind and how it functions, not necessarily to interfere with it at first, but simply to notice what you are thinking and how you are feeling. This takes practice.

Often when you encounter a negative thought or feeling you want to either indulge in it and intensify the feeling or destroy and eliminate the feeling. In the practice of Checking Your Attitude you will do neither. Instead, the goal is to establish an observer's neutrality. Ron Kurtz, author of Haikomi Therapy,[5] refers to this state as mindful awareness. You act very much like the doctor that is observing a slide under the microscope. When a doctor looks in the microscope the intent is to observe, not change what is there. After a careful examination, the doctor can decide what to do about what is observed. You are seeing what is going on, noticing it, but not trying to change it without thoughtful consideration.

---

[5] Haikomi Therapy, Ron Kurtz

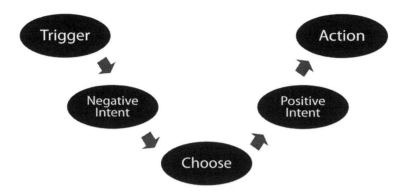

5 Steps To Check Your Attitude

There are five basic steps in making an attitude check and shifting from negative to positive intent.

Checking your Attitidude begins with awareness.

1. Identify what triggers you into a negative state of mind.

2. Identify which negative state of mind you go into.

3. Move into a Choice Point to neutralize the negative impact and open your mind to making a clear choice.

4. Choose Positive Intention as the basis for your thinking and feeling.

5. Move into action based on Positive Intention.

Obviously, you will have to practice this process over and over again until it becomes your new way of responding. Don't expect it to become habit immediately, and don't be discouraged when you slip back into your old patterns. You will be course correcting. Know that you always have the choice to assume Negative or Positive Intention at any time in any situation. Once you get a good practice going, when those opportunites arise to "go south," you will bounce back.

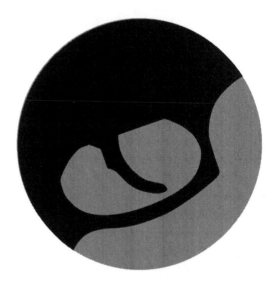

The Trigger—The Attitude Check

"Time stays long enough for anyone who will use it."
—Leonardo da Vinci

STEP ONE: Identify what triggers you

The Check Your Attitude process begins with becoming aware of what triggers you into a negative state/feeling. Triggers are automatic responses. In other words, they happen and you feel crappy seemingly instantly. Because they happen so fast they are elusive and reside in your blind spot. Triggers refer to what is called a negative anchored response. Because triggers are connected to a strong feeling you often just get wrapped up in the feeling and emotion and forget that there was something inside of you that created that response.

While the basic fight or flight responses are built into humans at the factory, you have a sophisticated overlay of responses that create ecstasy and misery. While it may seem convenient to ascribe your reactions to the world as someone else's creation, they are yours. You are the only person at the keyboard programming your internal computer. The facts are that you create your responses to stimuli in the world. Triggers are the things that you see or hear that are the primary stimulus of an automatic response. In order to discover what your triggers are you must take on a curious attitude about your reactions to things. Usually you have to discover your triggers backwards, meaning you start with the feeling and work back to what was the stimulus at the start of the process. To get there, ask yourself, "What was the thought that created that feeling?" and, "What happened right before that thought?" What happened right before your thought is usually the trigger.

Triggers take all sorts of forms and shapes. They usually revolve around the effect other people have on you that you don't seem to have any control over. Triggers can range from the way that somebody looks at you—a roll of the eyes, stern or disapproving look, looking away, shake of the head; to the way they say something—snippy, condescending, disapproving tone or words; to a little sound that they make— sighs, sucking of the teeth sounds, uhms, ahs; to a phrase or a set of words that they say to you.

When you get triggered you assume that your perception of the situation is true and accurate and that your bad feeling is caused by the external circumstances. Common phrases that you may hear are, "You made me angry," "She pissed me off," "They made me feel unwanted," "The phone is making me irritated." It feels like someone/they are doing something that "makes" you feel a certain way. When you are triggered into the Negative Intention Molecule, you feel the effect of what is going on. You feel exposed, vulnerable, and unable to protect yourself from what is happening. When you are triggered in this way you assume a Negative Intention and feel that your reaction is justified given their intention and actions.

Most of the time assuming Negative Intention is just that, an assumption that has not been verified. We call it a trigger because you go off half-cocked and ready to fire back. When you get triggered, the last thing on your mind is to check in with the other person to find out where he is really at. Usually when you are triggered in a negative way you automatically think about getting back at the person(adversarial revenge), or just feel demolished by what you think she said or did (victimized), or you may pretend to rise above by putting him in a lower position (Rescuer).

Become Aware of What Triggers You

Once you have developed awareness of your triggers, the next time you get triggered you can say to yourself, "I was just triggered. I am noticing my thoughts and feelings." You will see the pattern of how you get triggered rather than be the subject of the trigger. Having this observer's view of your thoughts is much different than the knee jerk response when you are triggered. When you become aware of what triggers you into a negative state you are one giant step ahead of where you were.

If you fail to identify the trigger in Checking Your Attitude you may not be able to create the change you desire. It's like using a weed whacker to cut off a weed versus pulling the weed out at its root. Identifying your trigger takes you to the root of your pattern, and that's where you need to go to make real change. Triggers have an impact because they are followed by the thoughts and feelings of negative intent. This is the meaning that you ascribe to the trigger.

STEP TWO: Identify Negative Intention

The trigger and the Negative Intention are close cousins to each other and happen almost simultaneously. When you assume Negative Intention you get upset. When you assume Negative Intention it creates a negative gut reaction. Negative Intention is the story that you tell yourself about the other person or situation. The Positive Intention of Negative Intention is to protect you from a perceived danger. If you say to yourself, "She is just out for herself," it is so you won't get hurt or continue to be hurt. It is a message that allows you to distance yourself from that person.

It's important to clarify the Negative Intention that you have assumed. In a sense the Negative Intention is very much part of the trigger. It is the automatic negative conclusions and feeling you have about that situation. What is your automatic thought? Is this person out to do you harm, to sabotage you, to mistreat you, to disrespect you? What is your automatic reaction to what was said or done? Usually a short phrase or image will come to you with a strong negative feeling that grabs your gut. Negative Intentions can sound like "He just wants to control the situation," "She doesn't like me," "He is ignoring me," "She is punishing me," "I am not as good as he is." See if you can actually put your finger on the negative thoughts you have when you are triggered.

Once you've identified the Negative Intention, identify what point in the Negative Intent Molecule it is being expressed. Are you in an adversarial state? Are in you in a victimized state? Are you in a rescuing mode? Once you know where you are on the molecule and by identifying your reaction you will better be able to neutralize the impact and make a change. Once again the goal is to be the witness; you are not trying to change or stop the pattern. If you try to extinguish the negative thought or feelings, they just go underground and will resurface. As you develop a neutral state of mind to observe, you are creating the place to make changes.

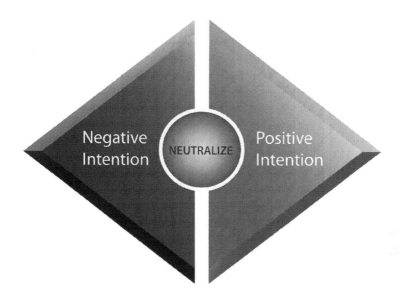

STEP THREE: Pause and Check and Choose

Step 3 is the step where you pause, reflect, and neutralize. Take a moment to review your process by asking yourself some questions: "What was it that triggered me? What were my Negative Intention thoughts and feelings?" The next step is to pause, check, and say, "Okay, where am I right now? I've assumed negative intent. I am assuming this person's out to get me. What am I defending myself from?" When you reflect on your process it allows you to separate yourself from it. When you can create some space around your negative pattern of thinking it helps to neutralize the associated negative feelings.

Neutralize

As odd as it may seem, it is often helpful at this step to take a deep breath. Your breathing is deeply connected with your feeling state, and taking a deep breath helps clear the emotional palette and calms the nervous system. When you neutralize, you reset the flight or fight physiology and restore the logical circuits in your brain. We are not talking about hyperventilating, but taking two or three good, deep breaths will help change your feeling state, increase the oxygen in your system, and actually help you think better.

Go ahead and try it right now: one...two...three...fill all the way up like you are filling your whole body to the very top of your head, then exhale, letting your lips come open and relaxing your jaw. Neutralizing allows you to let go of the Negative Intention that you have been holding on to from the past and imagine into your future. Neutralizing is letting go of the negative chatter inside of your head and letting everything come to a gentle pause.

Neutralizing is intentionally suspending the need to make a case against that person or situation. Neutralizing is letting go of being right about how wrong you think the other person is. Neutralizing is letting go of your right for revenge. Neutralizing is putting down your sword and shield and stepping away from the battle to be in a quiet place where no defense is necessary. It is relief.

Neutralizing is taking that moment to put the machinery of your mind in neutral. It is not forcing your mind in any way. You cannot coerce or force your mind into neutrality; it is something that you intentionally allow. Neutralizing is allowing more space in between your thoughts. It is a moment of meditative silence.

Your body will let you know you are neutralizing because you naturally will relax. Your mind relaxes and becomes quiet. Your body relaxes and becomes calm as you return to a peaceful center.

It is only when you allow your mind to completely quiet that you can truly choose. This choice point is represented by the circle in between the two molecules. You become aware of both possibilities of assuming good and Negative Intention. By letting your mind pause and letting go of the past, you no longer need to cling to Negative Intention to defend your feeling of being hurt. You no longer have to avoid but can choose freely.

It is a moment where you get to ask yourself, "What do you want for yourself?" "What is the direction you want your life to take?" "What is the experience of your life that you want to have?" Whatever the answer, you ask a follow-up question: "And if you had that, what you wanted, what experience would you have?" "And if you had that, what you wanted, what experience would you have?" You keep asking this question until you end up with a purely positive state of mind...and that leads you to the place where you will be ready to choose your Positive Intention and take a fresh look at the event of your life.

Good. Now you are ready to look at identifying the Positive Intention to reframe the situation that you are in into a positive context.

STEP FOUR: Choose Positive Intent

Choosing Positive Intent allows you to deal constructively with the specific situation at hand. What's the new thought that will replace the Negative Intention? One way to think about the Positive Intention of the other person is to ask yourself, "What is this person trying to accomplish that is for the greater good?" Some examples of Positive Intention may sound like:

- For someone who seems like she just wants to be right, the Positive Intention might be—she is trying to make the best decision.

- For someone who seems like a bully, the Positive Intention might be—he wants to hold his ground and not be taken advantage of.

- For someone who seems selfish, the Positive Intention might be—she is taking care of her own needs.

- For someone who raises his voice, the Positive Intention might be—he is concerned about failure.

- For someone who is stubborn, the Positive Intention might be—she wants to be sure before changing course.

- For someone who like to argue, the Positive Intention might be—he likes rigor, to be challenged, and/or he likes to find out how I think.

- For someone who complains, the Positive Intention might be—she is stuck and wants things to change but doesn't know how to make it happen.

You may have to take a moment to think about what the other person's Positive Intention might be. Sometimes you may not know exactly and you may have to make it up but that is okay. The purpose is to reset your mind so that you can take a positive course of action.

STEP FIVE: Take Action

Once you assume Positive Intention, identify where in the Positive Intent Molecule you want to be operating from. Use the Matrix to align your way of thinking and behaving (page 166).

You ask yourself:

Should I move to Visionary mode? Visionary behaviors include keeping the focus on goals, being passionate, committed, and resolved.

Should I go to Activator and focus on the process of how to get to the goal? Activator behaviors include setting the course of action/strategy that needs to take place, communicating, being accountable.

Should I go to Coach and think about people? Coach behaviors include providing guidance, empowering and motivating so people can be at their best.

More than likely you will pick a combination of the three for each situation. Once you pick, write down what specific thoughts and behaviors you will be demonstrating.

Now it is time to put it all together and take action. You are aware, you have shifted your attitude, and you have moved into positive intent. Action is the result!

The above five steps complete the attitude check. Notice the triggers causing the negative loop, clarify your Negative Intention, notice the drama involved, identify your persona on the negative intent molecule, pause and check what's going on, choose positive intent, and take action. You will get better and better at turning your negative loops into positive reactions instead of falling down into the negative spiral.

EXAMPLE

Let's take the example from page 58 of a negative loop and see how it can be "checked."

"I stood before the executive team, making a presentation. They all seem engaged and alert, except for Larry, who seemed bored out of his mind."

> ATTITUDE CHECK: Larry seems preoccupied. I wonder what is on his mind.

"He turned his dark, morose eyes away from me and **put his hand to his mouth to yawn.**"

> ATTITUDE CHECK: He must be exhausted. I wonder what has been keeping him up at night.

"He didn't ask any questions until I was almost done."

> ATTITUDE CHECK: He was listening to make sure he had the full data set.

"Then he interrupts with: 'I think we should ask for a full report.' In this work culture, that typically means, 'Let's move on.'"

ATTITUDE CHECK: He wants to keep the ball rolling because he thinks everyone understands and there are a couple of agenda items that he wants to make sure they cover.

"Everyone started to shuffle their papers and put their notes away. **Larry obviously thinks that I am incompetent, I muse**—which is a shame, because these ideas are exactly what his department needs."

ATTITUDE CHECK: I wonder what Larry thinks about what I presented. I will set up a debrief call to see what he is walking away with.

"Now that I think of it, he's never liked my ideas. Clearly, **Larry is a power-hungry jerk**."

ATTITUDE CHECK: I would like to have a better understanding of Larry's priorities and drivers.

"By the time I've returned to my seat, I've made a decision: I am not going to include anything in my report that Larry can use. He wouldn't read it, or, worse still, he'd just use it against me. **It is too bad I have an enemy who's so prominent in the company**."

ATTITUDE CHECK: I need to have a better relationship with Larry so we can be on the same page.

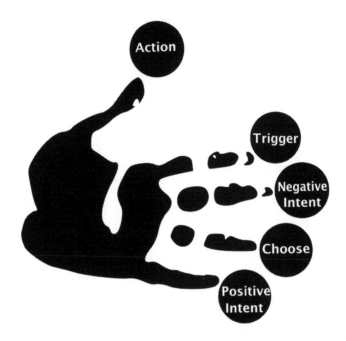

An easy way to remember the attitude check process is to use your hand. How? Let's review the Five Steps again.

1. First, identify the trigger. (This relates to the trigger or index finger on your hand.)

2. Second, your middle finger is your Negative Intention. This makes some literal sense!

3. The third step is pausing, checking, and choosing. That is your fourth finger.

4. The fourth step is the baby finger, and represents positive intent.

5. The fifth is the payoff, the thumbs up leadership position of taking positive action.

Practice moving from the Index finger (triggers) to the Middle Finger (negative intent) to the Fourth Finger (choice) to the Fifth finger (positive intent) to the Thumb (action, thumbs up) over and over to remind yourself how to check and transform your attitude. It will take time, but it is an excellent reminder. Use it throughout the day. You can practice it while watching TV. You can practice it while listening to the radio. You can definitely practice it in traffic. Use it when you are having things around you that are triggering you into negative behaviors. You can practice taking yourself through this attitude check, and when you are done, give yourself a thumbs up.

Here are some real life examples that illustrate triggers, negative intent, choosing, and positive intent. Add your own to each topic.

TRIGGERS: What happens outside of you to cause you to "trigger" a response.

Rolling of the eyes, looking away, someone saying something under their breath, criticism, pointing out what is missing, yawn, frown, negative tone in their voice, exasperating exhale, cold stare, frowning, head shaking "no."

NEGATIVE INTENT: What happens inside of you as you interpret the effect of the trigger.

They don't like me, they are bored, they don't value me, she hates me, I don't count, I am less than, he has it out for me, I don't measure up, this situation is impossible, it will never work, dumb ass.

CHOOSING: The place where you can reflect on your thinking and neutralize the impact of Negative Intention.

Oh, I can see now what I was doing, Wow, now I understand how negative I was thinking, I can see how I was making myself feel bad; my mind has been spinning like a rollercoaster. I am calm now.

POSITIVE INTENT: Your new attitude.

He is doing the best he can, she just wants things to be stable(unwilling to change), he wants the project to be successful (for someone who wants to be right), she wants to keep a strong focus (close minded), he adjust to the current situation (easily changes his mind).

> *"My mother's menu consisted of two choices:*
> *Take it or leave it."*
> **—Buddy Hackett**

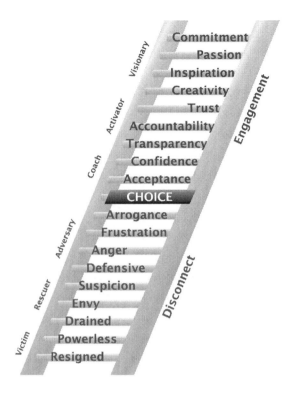

21. CHECK YOUR ATTITUDE LADDER

"The ladder of success is best climbed
by stepping on the rungs of opportunity."
—Ayn Rand

Another easy way to utilize these concepts and apply them is the Check Your Attitude Ladder. The Ladder is a linear way in which the molecules are stretched out into steps in the order of victim, rescuer, adversary, coach, activator, visionary. Using this visual it very easy to see at a glance whether you're operating from positive or negative intention. What rung are you on and in what direction are you going? If you are below the Choice line then it's time to do the Check Your Attitude process and get yourself into positive intention which will naturally engage you in the world. Simply take a step back, take a breath, and intentionally choose a positive mindset.

In addition to conversations we have with others, paying attention to the commentary inside of your head will give you cues as to whether you are above or below the line. Following are some examples to give you clues as to where you or others are operating from.

A fun way to deepen your understanding of each of these places on the ladder is to try saying the phrases out loud to yourself or with a friend to get a feel for each of these attitude states. You probably will find that you resonate with some more than others both above and below the choice line, and this will give you insights as to the elements of your personal mind molecules.

Resigned

- It's not going to or I don't make any difference.
- My efforts are useless.
- No matter what they/I do it's not going to make any difference.
- This whole thing is useless.
- This will never amount to much.

- The whole situation is the same old thing all over again, and we're going to end up right where we started.

Powerless

- I can't/they can't do anything about it.
- My boss can't do anything about it.
- No one has any authority.
- My boss/significant other won't let me.
- The whole situation is set up so that we can't really be successful.

Drained

- I'm exhausted.
- I've done everything I can.
- It has sucked the life out of me.
- This whole thing is sucking the life out of me.
- That person is a mood hoover, energy drain.

Envy

- She's/he's got everything.
- I wish I was as smart as he is
- He's the golden child.
- I wish I was working there, they have a much better office.
- I wish I had the money to dress like that.
- He/she just had it handed to them.
- Must be nice to have an office/car/other like that.

- If I had a boss like that, I'd be doing well too.

Suspicion

- He/she is up to something
- I don't think she likes me.
- She/he is really out to get me.
- I don't think they like people like me.
- I think they have something up their sleeve.

Defensive

- It's not my fault.
- It's their fault.
- The whole situation was set up for me/us to lose.
- This is not my problem.
- They're the ones that are to blame for this.
- Hey, I just work here.
- Look, we can't do anything about that.

Anger

- They really piss me off.
- The whole situation, this whole thing, is wrong.
- People don't step up to the challenge.
- I feel like management is just two-faced.

Frustration

- No matter what I do they won't budge.
- We can't get a decision.

- We just can't make the progress we want.
- That person is just being stubborn.
- They won't budge.
- They're just being closed-minded.
- They won't accept any new ideas.
- They are slow to take action.
- This needs to happen now.

Arrogance

- I know everything and they/you don't know any-thing.
- If they'd just listen to me they'd have the answer.
- They never come to us/me. We're the ones that are closest to the work being done.
- I know everything and they don't know shit.
- How long have I been here? Fifty years.
- Does anyone ever ask me what they should do? No.
- They just come up with their lofty ideas.
- They think they know all the answers, but they have no idea what is really going on.
- They should be asking us, the people that do the work, what we need to do.

Acceptance

- These are the cards that have been dealt.
- I need to move forward.
- We need to move forward.

- Look, this is the way things are right now. You need to make the best of it.
- I have my strengths and weaknesses.
- This is the situation that we need to deal with.

Confidence

- I/you/they/we can do it.
- I've/you've got the skills and abilities to make it happen.
- I may not know exactly how I'm going to make it happen, but I know that I'm going to make it happen.
- I trust that you can do it.
- Don't worry, it will turn out.
- We're going to get there.

Transparency

- Here's my thinking and how I arrived at my conclusions.
- What was your thinking and how did you get to that particular point of view?
- Let's make sure that we ask everyone what's going on for them.
- Here's my decision and here's how I arrived at that.
- Here's my conclusion and this is what my thinking was that allowed me to get here.
- What's your thinking, and how did you arrive at that conclusion?

- We need to find out how they made that decision.

Accountability

- I will do what I say I will do.
- Can I count on you to do what you say you're going to do?
- Everyone needs to step up and keep their word.
- Here's what I'm going to do and I will do it.
- You said what you would do.
- Have you done it? When will you?
- They're counting on us to keep our word.

Trust

- I will do what I say I will do.
- You're trustworthy.
- We can trust what's going on here.
- I know what my intentions are.
- I know what your intentions are.
- I know that they have good intentions.
- I know that the situation may not be optimum, but they really want us to win.

Creativity

- I'm stepping out of the box.
- That was a great idea.
- We need to ask the questions that haven't been asked yet.

- I've got a great idea.
- That's a great idea.
- Let's step out of the box and see what we can think of.
- What are the questions that we haven't asked yet?

Inspiration

- Let's do this.
- This is a great opportunity that we have.
- I really want to go there.
- What he said really engaged me in wanting to go there.

Passion

- I got skin in the game.
- They're fully committed.
- I really want to make this a winner.
- I am really excited about working on this project.
- I think we're making great progress.
- That was a phenomenal thing that you did and it really got us moving.

Commitment

- I/we will do what it takes.
- Let's make this win.
- I'm going to do whatever it takes to get there.
- Let's do whatever it takes to get there.
- Nothing will stop us from getting there.

22. COACHING WITH THE GROW MODEL

At work the GROW model is a great tool that you can use to assist others in identifying where they are and how to get going in the right direction:

G – Goal: "Where do you want to be?"

R – Reality: "Where are you now?" (More than likely you will start here then ask them about their goal.)

R – Responsibility: "What has been your role in this situation being this way?

O – Options: "What are your options to reach your goal?"

W – Will: What are you going to do? What is your commitment?"

By just asking them the GROW questions you can begin a simple and powerful coaching process. My other book, *Daring to Have Real Conversations at Work*, has tips on having these types of conversations.

"I hope our wisdom will grow with our power, and teach us, that the less we use our power the greater it will be."
—Thomas Jefferson

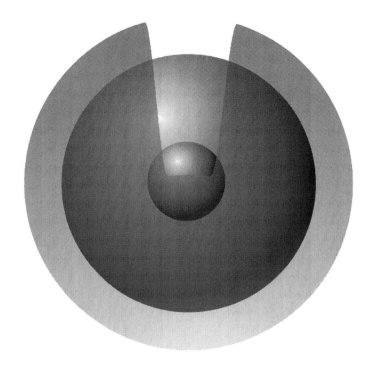

23. ACTING FROM YOUR CORE

A small body of determined spirits fired by an unquenchable
faith in their mission can alter the course of history.
—Mahatma Gandhi

Your core values are a set of principles that guide how you think and behave. You won't give up on your core values even when times are tough. Your values generally instill a sense of wholeness and make you feel good. They are qualities that you hold deep within you that feel sacred.

Your values determine what you think is right and wrong. Your values motivate you and are the guideposts for how you live your life. When they are being fulfilled they give you the most joy and when they are being violated they give you the most anguish. Having a clear sense of your core values also makes it easier to maintain an attitude of Positive Intention.

In this chapter you will identify your core values molecule, the three elements that are core to your life.

Knowing other people's values can be useful when you want to get and hold their attention and/or influence them. Understanding the differences in values in people is also a foundation for appreciation, or a reason to dissociate. For example, people who are corrupt, dishonest, and undependable have chosen a different value system than people who are honest and keep their word.

Practice the following Values Discovery Exercise. After you complete the process you will have a good sense of your core values. Try the process with your friends, family, and work associates and learn what makes them tick.

VALUES DISCOVERY EXERCISE

Follow the instructions on the next page.

Achievement
Accountability/ Responsibility
Acknowledgment
Advancement
Adventure
Affection(caring)
Appreciation
Arts
Challenging problems
Change and Variety
Choice
Close relationships
Communication
Community
Competition
Conformity
Control
Cooperation
Country
Creativity
Decisiveness
Democracy
Diversity
Ecological awareness
Economic security
Effectiveness
Efficiency
Ethical practice
Excellence
Excitement
Expertise
Faith
Fame
Family
Fast living
Fast-pacedwork

Financial gain
Freedom
Friendships
Fun
God
Growth
Health
Helping others
Honesty
Humor
Improvement
Inclusion
Independence
Influencing others
Inner harmony
Integrity
Intellectual status
Involvement
Job tranquility
Knowledge
Leadership
Leisure
Learning
Location
Love
Loyalty
Magic
Meaningful work
Merit
Money
Nature
Being around people who are open and honest
Order
Passion
Patience
Personal development

Physical challenge
Pleasure
Power and Authority
Privacy
Public service
Purity
Quality of what I take part in
Quality relationships
Respect
Religion
Reputation
Results
Security
Self-Respect
Serenity
Service
Sophistication
Spiritual Focus
Stability
Status
Supervising others
Teaching
Thinking
Time freedom
Transformation
Tranquility
Trust
Truth
Urgency
Wealth
Winning
Wisdom
Work under pressure
Work with others
Working alone

VALUES DISCOVERY EXERCISE

1. Look at the preceding list of words and choose about ten that appeal to you. Go with your first gut response. If you want to add a word of your own that is not on the list, please do so.

2. Now choose your top three words. These represent your top three values. Take your time (this can take up to ten minutes). Notice how you sorted the words to come to your final top three.

3. Jot down your top three. What do these words mean to you? Really take some time to feel how they touch you emotionally and intellectually.

4. Reflect on the events of your life to identify when and where these values took root.

5. Now go deeper. What personal story wraps around these words? What people influenced you in some why to choose these values? What events catalyzed your choices?

6. What does it feel like to live your values at work and at home? How does it affect your ability to make decisions? How does it affect your relationships?

7. What is it like when you are not living your values fully? What is the quality of your decision

making? What is the quality of your relationships at home and at work?

8. What can you do to strengthen your ability to live from your values? When will you do this?
   In this chapter you will identify your core values molecule, the three elements that are core to your life.

9. Fill in your three core values and the elements that connect them. Take your time to decide on the connecting elements, and make this a work in progress. As you develop your Core Values Molecule you will find that it represents a deep natural strength that you can count on.

24. ESTABLISHING YOUR PERSONAL PURPOSE IN LIFE

"I have found that among its other benefits,
giving liberates the soul of the giver."
—Maya Angelou

PURPOSE

Each of us has a purpose. Each of us is meant to be here and to be of service to each another. You are unique, and you bring qualities into this world that nobody else can contribute. Your purpose in life is born out of your values and describes how you engage with the world and the results that ensue. When you clarify your purpose in life it tunes or calibrates your internal barometer so that you can always adjust your thinking and actions to be in alignment. When you know your purpose you have a place to refer to, a home base that is solid, yet grows as you do. When you are operating in alignment with your purpose there is a flow, an energy, that is fulfilled from the inside out.

DEFINING YOUR PURPOSE

Your purpose in life is not necessarily defined by an occupation. And please note, there is no right or wrong purpose in life. Your purpose expresses your values and makes you feel good about being alive. Think of your purpose in terms of the following two primary questions:

- What activity would you like to engage in with other people that would bring them a benefit?

- What activity would bring you great satisfaction as well?

Remember, the key to the answer is that you and the other people will feel inspired, enlivened, and energized by this activity. When you think about your purpose in life it may be just a general purpose for all human beings, or it can be for a specific group.

Your purpose in life can be expressed as a statement. To formulate your verbal purpose it is important to identify three key elements.

1. "Who" do you want to address? Are you trying to include everyone or a specific group?

2. "How" do you want to interact with them?

3. What is the "result." What is the payoff of your purpose?

For example, "My life purpose is to help(HOW) children (WHO) by creating environments to allow them to learn and grow (RESULT)." Here are some more examples to get you started. Remember, your purpose needs to make you feel energized, uplifted, and alive.

My purpose in life is...

1—to work with the elderly population to help them lead fulfilling lives.

2—to serve God in all my actions.

3—to create environments at work that enhance creativity, productivity while enhancing job satisfaction.

4—to help people become financially secure.

5—to help people express themselves through singing to contribute to their leading happy lives.

6—to guide people to find their spiritual self.

7—to coach leaders to be more effective.

8—to help people with handicaps lead fulfilling lives.

When I first created my purpose I came up with some statement like healing the sick and, you know, being of service. The truth is, as well meaning as they sounded, my purpose points didn't give me a lot of energy. I realized that I needed to be more "me," and I had to admit what it is I really enjoy doing is having fun with people. I enjoy bringing lightness to things. So I recreated my statement and said, "I want to bring people (who) fun and joy and laughter (what) to make their lives fulfilling and growth oriented (result)." I knew it was true for me because it felt engaging and vibrant. It's important to note that your purpose will evolve and take many forms over time. It goes deeper. My purpose in life on the deepest level to serve God. My deepest purpose permeates all aspects of my life. My deepest purpose translates in my work as: To inspire and empower people to bring their full energy to life!

"The best way to find yourself is to lose yourself
in the service of others."
—Mohandas Gandhi

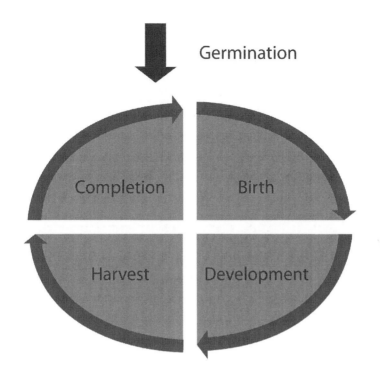

Germination

Completion

Birth

Harvest

Development

25. LIVING YOUR VISION

"Great thoughts speak only to the thoughtful mind, but great actions speak to all mankind."
—Theodore Roosevelt

Once you determine your values and craft your purpose statement, you will begin to live your life in alignment with your purpose. As your commitment to living your purpose grows, you will find that you will be living your vision. More and more visions will come to you that will help you and others. You are not limited to having one vision in your life. In fact, most people live several visions in their lives. This process of visioning goes through distinct cycles and phases.

GERMINATION OF YOUR VISION

The first phase is germination. The germination of a vision takes place deep within you and often, once the vision is germinating, you may feel it but not know exactly what it is. It's a sense that something's coming but you don't know what it's going to look like, yet somehow you know that there's going to be a change. It even may get to the point of being quite disconcerting because reality today doesn't seem quite right and you can't really put your finger on what's up. This might feel like limbo but it is very ripe with what will be. You cannot speed up the germination phase. There's no way to kind of hurry it up any more than it's possible to hurry the birth of a baby. During this time you are usually able to communicate with friends and your inner circle of colleagues about this vague but real sensation, but nothing is concrete...yet.

BIRTH OF YOUR VISION

The second phase is the birth of the vision. As you are moving into the birthing phase things become clearer. You begin to see some details and your vision begins to come into focus. This is when it's useful to sit down and begin writing things down. Keep a Vision Journal and jot down the what's, the when's, the where's, the who's involved. You can refer to Chapter 17 on the Visionary to find more inspiration. Your conversations will shift to, "I think _____ is coming. It's becoming clearer to me. It's not fully baked yet, but I know it's very close to the horizon." As you become more in touch with what's just out of reach you are able to birth this wonderful new reality.

DEVELOPMENT OF YOUR VISION

The third phase is the development of your vision. The development of a vision can take from weeks to decades, depending on its scope and magnitude. This is when you can jump into the Activator position and begin to take the reins and organize the development of the vision by assigning roles and responsibilities, deadlines, and details in terms of how you are really going to be moving toward this particular goal. Now you are playing both Activator and Visionary. As the Visionary you keep things focused on the ultimate big picture as well as acknowledge the challenges and resistance that naturally will arise as progress is made.

As your vision unfolds you will see that there are many inadvertent benefits that are gained. These are called "precessional" effects. A precessional effect is an unexpected positive benefit impact that happens at ninety degrees to the direction that is being taken. For instance, seemingly inadvertently, the honey bee goes about its business of gathering honey. At ninety degrees to his body and his flight path, his legs gather pollen from one flower and "accidentally" take this pollen to the next flower, resulting in cross pollination. The outcome of this seemingly inadvertent accidental activity is that the bee contributes enormously to life on earth. You get pollination, the growth of crops, the sustaining of life for humans and animals.

Several years ago I owned a company that produced a personal growth weekend seminar called The Sage Experience. It took about 30 volunteers to produce a seminar for 100 participants. Soon it was discovered that the assistants received a great deal of value by assisting. They learned life skills and had many personal insights and development opportunities that made assisting as valuable as, if not more valuable than, taking the seminar itself. This is a form of precessional pay off.

HARVEST OF YOUR VISION

Harvest is when the vision is coming to fruition. It becomes clear to you and others that the goals of the vision are becoming fulfilled. Like development, the Harvest phase can last a lifetime.

COMPLETION OF YOUR VISION

The final stage of completion is when this vision is complete. It may be that things become systematized and you are playing the roles that are appropriate for you and others. It's happened and it works! Now you are ready for the next vision to come along (and it will) and the cycle begins again.

"Thinking is easy, acting is difficult, and to put one's thoughts into action is the most difficult thing in the world."
—Johann Wolfgang von Goethe

26. PERSONAL CHANGE MANAGEMENT

Shirley and George finished reading *Check Your Attitude at the Door*. They got a lot of value from immersing themselves in the narrative and processes, but each wanted a deeper experience. They both chose to take the one-day Check Your Attitude course. Afterward, each of them took a very different path.

SHIRLEY

Shirley bought herself a nice journal and kept it close by so that she could actively "work" the book. She made a conscious effort to practice and apply what she learned each week. She also went back through the book and answered all of the questions at the end of chapters. As she wrote in her journal, Shirley paid close attention to her thought patterns and then reviewed the types of thoughts that she was having. She noticed that she had many more limiting patterns than she initially realized.

Shirley decided to see if the tools and tips really worked. She checked her attitude several times a day and utilized the five steps to practice shifting her attitude (page 187). In a short time, Shirley was delighted to recognize how quickly she could shift from negative to positive intention.

Shirley also decided to share her process with Steve, a close friend. She asked, "Can you tell me what you think about what I'm doing?" Steve appreciated the opportunity to learn about Shirley's process and also discovered a good deal about his own thinking patterns as well. They decided to get together weekly for coffee. Shirley took her journal out and they would practice the exercises at the end of each chapter. Pretty soon, Steve actively applied the Check Process himself.

Shirley particularly liked creating her own version of the positive and negative molecules (see pages 168–171). She got inspired and came up with six different positive intention modules, three for at work and three for at home. Once those were done, she began to focus on how she could consciously turn situations around, create positive molecules, and pass them on to people in her life. If she saw somebody in a bad mood she would take out her chart and ask, "What are you experiencing right now? What's the negative intention that you're assuming? How can you neutralize it? How can you turn it into a positive intention and choose a positive behavior?"

Shirley found that she really enjoyed coaching those around her. At the end of three months, she found that her attitude was naturally based in positive intention and that people around her were experiencing it as well. Life ran more smoothly.

GEORGE

George's story, on the other hand, has a different ending. After George took the course he felt motivated but failed to implement the numerous tips and processes to follow up. He let time go by and eventually lost touch with the material that inspired him. At work the next couple of weeks, George found himself reacting negatively in numerous situations. He knew things weren't right but he couldn't quite remember how to go through the processes he had read about. As a matter of fact, he never once reviewed any of the chapters in the book.

George found himself in more and more negative moods, but instead of making positive changes, he beat himself up. He would reprimand himself and in a critical tone would tell himself, "I've been through this course and I'm not applying it. What a loser." George fell into the most common pitfall beginners experience when trying to make personal changes he felt guilty about not following through.

George simply hadn't practiced the processes he had learned about. If he had just dipped into the appropriate chapters he could have easily recognized that he had assumed negative intent and could walk himself through the process to get to positive intent. Instead, he got into negative intent about his negative intent. George felt so discouraged from his seeming failure that he perpetuated his self-doubt and fell into a deeper state of negative intent. As the weeks went by, George failed to turn to the processes in the book that addressed his condition and instead felt lower. At that point he was too embarrassed to even consider getting some help. It never occurred to George that he could ask Shirley, his business colleague, how she was applying what she learned in the course. He was too humiliated to find himself hovering in his negative place, embarrassed and ashamed.

George was a perfect poster boy for pitfalls to Self Change Management. Had he simply gone to Shirley and confessed, "You know, I find myself in negative intent and I don't really know what to do," things could have changed for the better. If George was just able to articulate his condition and needs out loud he would be taking the first step toward transforming his negative intent and would also create a coaching opportunity for Shirley. Instead, George stubbornly went off the deep end. After one month, he was in such a bad mood at work that his home life started to suffer as well. George fell into the three pitfalls of personal change management:

1. Assuming you will remember what you learned.

2. Feeling guilty about falling off track.

3. Feeling embarrassed about asking for help.

The moral of the story is actually up to you. After reading this book or going to the seminar (or both), make sure you focus on the key elements of personal change management. They are:

1. Practice, practice, practice. Focus on a chapter a week.

2. Complete the exercises at the end of each chapter. Use a journal.

3. Share your work/insights with a friend.

4. Share your work/insights at work.

5. Ask for coaching and be a coach for others.

Remember, you are developing a whole new muscle. There is a learning curve, but once you get the hang of it, you'll be amazed at how easily you can apply your new learning and implement your tangible tools. The bottom line is, everyone falls off the wagon sometime. It's normal. Just don't beat yourself up when you do. It's really a great opportunity to practice, practice, practice. Try saying, "Oh, I just fell off the wagon and now I can use this situation to get back on track with myself and back into positive intent. It's time to check my attitude at the door and create the reality at home and at work that I want to inhabit."

This last example of attitude is an adaptation of one of Steve Jobs' inventions, the AttitudePod. Everyone has a built-in AttitudePod.

Some ideas to think about:

- Your circle wheel lets you choose between positive or negative tracks.
- Ever watch someone who is listening to their iPod and the mood they are in?
- What's the background soundtrack to the different situations you face at work and otherwise?
- What does your playlist look like?
- What filters do you look at reality through?
- What mood does your playlist put you in?

- When unexpected things happen, what happens to your attitude?
- What are your favorites?
- What decisions about handling situations do you pre-make? How might this create a blind spot for you?
- Are some songs stuck on repeat?
- Ever see someone whose music is so loud you can hear it even though they have earphones on?
- Ever get *their* song stuck in your head?
- Ever talk to someone but you can tell they are listening to their own tracks, not you?
- When is the volume on your pod so loud you lose touch?
- What tracks do you have that put you in a bad mood? What's the melody? Lyrics?
- As you look around at people, ask yourself, "What kind of tracks are they listening to?" especially if they are in a really good mood or really bad mood.
- We all have an attitude soundtrack. It is your choice. What are you going to choose as you walk through the door?

"Your time is limited, so don't waste it living someone else's life. Don't let the noise of others' opinions drown out your own inner voice. And most important, have the courage to follow your heart and intuition."
—Steve Jobs

27. WHAT IS NEXT?

Once there lived a village of creatures along the bottom of a great crystal river. Each creature in its own manner clung tightly to the twigs and rocks of the river bottom, for clinging was their way of life, and resisting the current is what each had learned from birth. But one creature said at last, "I trust that the current knows where it is going. I shall let go, and let it take me where it will. Clinging, I shall die of boredom."

The other creatures laughed and said, "Fool! Let go, and that current you worship will throw you tumbled and smashed across the rocks, and you will die quicker than boredom!"

But the one heeded them not, and taking a breath did let go, and at once was tumbled and smashed by the current across the rocks. Yet, in time, as the creature refused to cling again, the current lifted him free from the bottom, and he was bruised and hurt no more.

And the creatures downstream, to whom he was a stranger, cried, "See a miracle! A creature like ourselves, yet he flies! See the Messiah, come to save us all!" And the one carried in the current said, "I am no more Messiah than you. The river's delight is to lift us free, if only we dare let go. Our true work is this voyage, this adventure. (Story from Illusions: The Adventures of a Reluctant Messiah, Richard Bach)

And so it is...as you get into the rhythm of Checking Your Attitude you will create greater freedom to enjoy life and to share this enjoyment and satisfaction with others. Expect to be challenged by the events of your day and the people in your life. Take joy in the challenge, for each challenge is an opportunity for you to Check Your Attitude and choose a positive way of interacting with the world to create a positive result.

Listen to the story you are telling about what happens in your life. You always have a choice to tell it from Positive or Negative Intention, and it is never too late to stop midstream and switch to Positive Intention. Taking that moment to choose Positive Intention will make a world of difference.

Ultimately, your goal is to enjoy each and every moment to the fullest. It is about feeling whole and fulfilled so that when you get to the very end of your life and you're taking your last breath, you can look back on your entire life and say to yourself, "I have no regrets. I've lived a full complete life."

"There comes a time when the mind takes a higher plane of knowledge but can never prove how it got there."
—Albert Einstein

APPENDIX

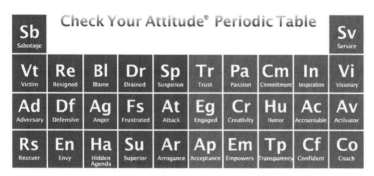

Mind Molecule Definitions

Below are definitions for each of the key elements of the mind molecules for your reference.

vic·tim

Etymology: Latin *victima*; perhaps akin to Old High German *wīh* holy Date: 15th century

1: a person who is deceived or cheated, as by his or her own emotions or ignorance, by the dishonesty of others, or by some impersonal agent

2: one that is subjected to oppression, hardship, or mistreatment

3: one that is tricked or duped

"They took advantage of my good will."

Victims think and feel that wrong is being done to them and they are powerless to do anything about it.

The Positive Intention of victims is that they want to change but are stuck and either don't know how to change or do not think they can change.

drained

Etymology: Middle English *draynen*, from Old English *drēahnian* Date: before 12th century

1: to deprive of strength; tire

2: to cause the gradual disappearance of

3: to exhaust physically or emotionally

4: lessen markedly in quantity, content, power, or value

"That person totally drained me."

One feels drained when they think that they have to give agreement to someone else's way of thinking or behaving.

Often occurs when you put up with someone rather than confront them.

The Positive Intention of drained is you want to reach a goal but lose sight of the goal and give up to the present circumstances because you don't have an effective way to deal with what is happening.

re·signed

Etymology: Middle English, from Anglo-French *resigner*, from Latin *resignare*, literally, to unseal, cancel, from *re-* + *signare* to sign, seal

Date: 14th century

1: to give (oneself) over without resistance

2: to give up deliberately; *especially*: to renounce by a formal act

3: to give up one's office or position: QUIT

4: to accept something as inevitable: SUBMIT

"I give up. That is just the way it is."

One resigns when they give up on any possibility of change. It is the home base for the Victim.

The Positive Intention of resigned is to recognize the original goal and reenergize. Look at the problem from the future and other angles and see what possible solutions might emerge.

at·tack

Etymology: Middle French *attaquer*, from Old Italian **estaccare*, to attach, from *staccastake*, of Germanic origin; akin to Old English *staca*

Date: 1562

1: to assail with unfriendly or bitter words

2: to begin to affect or to act on injuriously

3: to set upon or work against forcefully

4: to threaten with immediate capture

You attack and feel attacked when you are not taking full responsibility for what is happening.

The Positive Intention of attack is it is an opportunity to discover what the root causes are of the problem and to fix them.

ad·ver·sary

Date: 14th century

1: a person, group, or force that opposes or attacks; opponent; enemy; foe

2: a person, group, etc., that is an opponent in a contest; contestant

3: the Adversary, the devil; Satan

Adversary is the epitome of not taking responsibility.

The Positive Intention of the adversary is they are convinced, committed, and know what they want. It is a matter of discovering how they arrived at their conclusions.

an·ger

Date: 13th century

1: a strong feeling of displeasure and belligerence aroused by a wrong; wrath; ire

2: a strong emotion; a feeling that is oriented toward some real or supposed grievance

3: A strong feeling of displeasure, hostility or antagonism toward someone or something, usually combined with an urge to harm

4: Pain or stinging

5: To cause such a feeling of antagonism

Anger results when you are not getting your way. Underneath anger is fear of failure.

The Positive Intention of anger is that it energizes the situation and can be utilized if directed toward the goal.

de·fen·sive

Date: 14th century

1: excessively concerned with guarding against the real or imagined threat of criticism, injury to one's ego, or exposure of one's shortcomings.

2: devoted to resisting or preventing aggression or attack

3: of or relating to the attempt to keep an opponent from scoring in a game or contest

"That is not my problem." "If it weren't for _____ we would not be in this situation."

You become defensive when you want to deflect responsibility for any part of a situation. The second part of being defensive is assigning blame to someone or something else.

The Positive Intention of defensive is saving face. The defensive needs a way to accept mistakes and the wisdom that comes from learning from them.

frus·trat·ed

Etymology: Middle English, from Latin *frustratus*, past participle of *frustrare* to deceive, frustrate, from *frustra* in error, in vain

Date: 15th century

1: to balk or defeat in an endeavor

2: to induce feelings of discouragement

3: to make ineffectual: bring to nothing

4: Impede, obstruct

5: to make invalid or of no effect

"I am so frustrated that they won't agree with the plan."

You become frustrated when things continue to not going your way and you continue to insist on them going your way. It is a way of trying to be right rather than adjusting and doing the right thing.

The Positive Intention of frustrated is the commitment to achieve results.

ar·ro·gance

Origin: 1275-1325; Middle English < Middle French < Latin *arrogantia* presumption.

1: offensive display of superiority or self-importance; overbearing pride.

2: making claims or pretensions to superior importance or rights; overbearingly assuming; insolently proud.

res·cue

Etymology: Middle English *rescouen, rescuen*, from Anglo-French *rescure*, from *re-* + *escure* to shake off, from Latin *excutere*, from *ex-* + *quatere* to shake

Date: 14th century

1: to free from confinement, danger, or evil

2: save, deliver

3: to recover by force

"I had to step in." You rescue when you judge others as incapable and choose not to teach. Giving them the fish vs. teaching how to fish.

The Positive Intention of rescuing is wanting to help.

en·vy

Origin: 1250–1300; (noun) Middle English *envie* < Old French < Latin *invidia*, equivalent to *invid(us)* envious (derivative of *invidēre* to envy; see invidious) + *-ia* -y³; (v.) Middle English *envien* < Old French *envier* < Medieval Latin *invidiāre*, derivative of Latin *invidia*

1: a feeling of discontent or covetousness with regard to another's advantages, success, possessions, etc.

2: an object of envious feeling: *Her intelligence made her theenvy of her classmates.*

3: *Obsolete.* ill will.

4: to regard with envy; be envious of: *He envies her the position she has achieved in her profession.*

su·pe·ri·or

Etymology: Middle English, from Middle French, from Latin, comparative of *superus* upper, from *super* over, above

Date: 14th century

1: of higher rank, quality, or importance

2: courageously or serenely indifferent (as to something painful or disheartening)

3: greater in quantity or numbers <escaped by superior speed> b: excellent of its kind : better <her superior memory>

4: more comprehensive <a genus is superior to a species>

5: affecting or assuming an air of superiority

"Good thing I am around to get the job done, they just aren't up to it."

Superior is when you put others down so that you feel important, one-up, and necessary.

The Positive Intention of superior is to create a coaching opportunity to share your knowledge and expertise with others.

sa·bo·tage

Origin: 1865–70; < French, equivalent to *sabot(er)* to botch, orig., to strike, shake up, harry, derivative of *sabot* sabot + -*age* -age

1: any underhand interference with production, work, etc., in aplant, factory, etc., as by enemy agents during wartime or by employees during a trade dispute.

2: any undermining of a cause.

hidden agenda

Date: 1971 1: an ulterior motive

"I will show him who is better." "I will make sure everyone knows how bad she is."

You have a hidden agenda when you intentionally hide your motives and intention from others. Hidden agendas are one of the key elements involved in manipulating people.

The Positive Intention of hidden agenda is the opportunity to deepen the relationship and provide support of their goals and ask for help with your goals.

sus·pi·cion

Etymology: Middle English *suspecioun*, from Anglo-French, from Latin *suspicion-*, *suspicio*, from *suspicere* to suspect

Date: 14th century

1: the act or an instance of suspecting something wrong without proof or on slight evidence

2: mistrust

3: a state of mental uneasiness and uncertainty; doubt

Suspicion occurs when you assume that someone is guilty or has Negative Intentions but are unwilling to have a Real Conversation with them to talk about your perceptions and discover their intentions.

The Positive Intention of suspicion is the opportunity to deepen the relationship.

vi·sion·ary

Date: 1648

1: having or marked by unusually keen foresight and imagination

2: able or likely to see a future goal or condition that may seem unattainable or impractical from the perspective of today

3: able to see what is coming when there is not any present evidence

Step back and look at the big picture, where you are going, the final destination. Deal with details and remember to look at things from a higher altitude.

pas·sion

Etymology: late ME < ML *passiōnātus,* equiv. to LL *passiōn* passion + L *-ātus* -ate

Date: 14th-15th century

1: having, compelled by, or ruled by intense emotion or strong feeling; fervid

2: expressing, showing, or marked by intense or strong feeling; emotional: *passionate language.*

3. intense or vehement, as emotions or feelings: *passionate grief.*

5. easily moved to anger; quick-tempered; irascible.

Feel your passion and others will share it with you. You are a conduit for energy to flow through you. Make it intentional for people to be energized in your presence.

com·mit

Etymology: Middle English *committen*, from Anglo-French *committer*, from Latin *committereto* connect, entrust, from *com- + mittere* to send

Date: 14th century

1: to put into charge or trust, entrust

2: to pledge or assign to some particular course or use to pledge (oneself) to a position on an issue or question; express one's intention, feeling, etc.

3: to bind or obligate, as by pledge or assurance; pledge

4: to entrust, esp. for safekeeping; commend

5: to carry into action deliberately

Commitment gives you confidence to face the future. When you commit you are steeping into the future and taking a stand for creating your vision or the goal. People respond positively when they hear and see your commitment. It creates the space for contribution.

ser·vice

Origin: before 1100; Middle English (noun) < Old French < Latin *servitium* servitude, equivalent to *serv(us)* slave + *-itium* -ice; replacing Middle English *servise*, late Old English *serfise* ceremony < Old French *servise*, variant of *service* servicet

1: an act of helpful activity; help; aid. ready to be of help or use to someone, to be helpful or useful.

2: the organized system of apparatus, appliances, employees, etc., for supplying some accommodation.

Service is putting others before you. It is giving support generously and without the expectation for return. When you are of service to another you are willing to be selfless and willing to contribute to others without the need for praise or thanks.

trans·par·ent

Etymology: Middle English, from Medieval Latin *transparent-*, *transparens*, present participle of *transparēre* to show through, from Latin trans- +*parēre* to show oneself

Date: 15th century

1: free from pretense or deceit, frank

2: easily detected or seen through, obvious

3: readily understood

4: characterized by visibility or accessibility of information especially concerning business practices

Being transparent allows for a greater level of trust. People don't have to wonder. If you have an issue you clear it up in the moment. You let people know what you are up to.

ac·ti·vate

Date: 1626

1: to excite, make active; cause to function or act

2: to set up or formally institute with the necessary personnel and equipment

3: to make reactive or more reactive

4: to put an individual or unit on active duty

Activate, don't procrastinate. Take action now to move toward the goal. Get people excited about taking action. Assign roles and responsibilities. Be in rapport and keep the tempo up and encourage people to do new things.

cre·a·tiv·i·ty

Date: 1678

1: the ability to transcend traditional ideas, rules, patterns, relationships, or the like, and to create meaningful new ideas, forms, methods, interpretations, etc.; originality, progressiveness, or imagination

2: having the quality of something created rather than imitated

3: managed so as to get around conventional limits

"That team really thinks outside the box."

Creativity is when you think unconventionally to solve a problem or come up with an idea or expression. Get yourself and others to think about different angles to solve their problems.

ac·count·a·ble

Date: 14th century

1: able to answer for one's conduct and obligations, responsible

2: liable to be called to account as the primary cause, motive, or agent

3: being the cause or explanation

4: liable to review or in case of fault to penalties

5: able to choose for oneself between right and wrong, trustworthy

Step up and take full accountability and others will follow your example. Once you take full accountability you can uncover root causes for problems rather than just trying to CYA.

hu·mor

Etymology: Middle English *humour*, from Anglo-French *umor, umour*, from Medieval Latin & Latin; Medieval Latin *humor*, from Latin *humor, umor* moisture; akin to Old

Date: 14th century

1: characteristic or habitual cheerful temperament, disposition or bent

2: something that is or is designed to be comical or amusing

3: the mental faculty of discovering, expressing, or appreciating the ludicrous or absurdly incongruous that quality which appeals to a sense of the ludicrous or absurdly incongruous

Humor refreshes and recharges us. Self-deprecating humor is the best. Get people to laugh at you and they will be for you.

coach

Etymology: Middle English *coche*, from Middle French, from German *Kutsche*, from Hungarian *kocsi* (*szekér*), literally, wagon from *Kocs*, Hungary

Date: 1556

1: person who trains an athlete or a team of athletes

2: a private tutor who prepares a student for an examination

3: a person who instructs an actor or singer

Look for those opportunities to teach rather than take over. Think of questions that you can ask to get others to think for themselves.

em·pow·ers

Date: 1648

1: to give official authority or legal power to

2: enable

3: to promote the self-actualization or influence of

Push decision making to the lowest level that you can in your organization. Take calculated risks by letting people make their own decisions so they can learn.

trust

Etymology: Middle English, probably of Scandinavian origin; akin to Old Norse *traust* trust; akin to Old English *trēowe* faithful — more at TRUE

Date: 13th century

1: assured reliance on the character, ability, strength, or truth of someone or something

2: one in which confidence is placed, care or custody

3: dependence on something future or contingent, hope

4: a charge or duty imposed in faith or confidence or as a condition of some relationship

5: something committed or entrusted to one to be used or cared for in the interest of another

Treat people like they are trustworthy. Give them the opportunity to step up and deliver.

con·fi·dent

Etymology: Latin *confident-*, *confidens*, from present participle of *confidere*

Date: circa 1567

1: full of conviction: certain 2: having or showing assurance and self-reliance

Recognize and acknowledge the strengths that you see in other people. Develop their strengths rather than focus on their weaknesses.

Attitude Scorecard

Rate yourself at work, at home, and in your relationships.

CHECK YOUR ATTITUDE SCORE CARD		
RATING		**SCORE**
Suspicion -5 -4 -3 -2 -1 <> 1+ 2+ 3+ 4+ 5+ Trust		____
Blame -5 -4 -3 -2 -1 <> 1+ 2+ 3+ 4+ 5+ Commitment		____
Angry -5 -4 -3 -2 -1 <> 1+ 2+ 3+ 4+ 5+ Humor		____
Drained -5 -4 -3 -2 -1 <> 1+ 2+ 3+ 4+ 5+ Passionate		____
Arrogance -5 -4 -3 -2 -1 <> 1+ 2+ 3+ 4+ 5+ Acceptance		____
Resigned -5 -4 -3 -2 -1 <> 1+ 2+ 3+ 4+ 5+ Inspired		____
Defensive -5 -4 -3 -2 -1 <> 1+ 2+ 3+ 4+ 5+ Accountable		____
Hidden Agenda -5 -4 -3 -2 -1 <> 1+ 2+ 3+ 4+ 5+ Transparent		____
Envy -5 -4 -3 -2 -1 <> 1+ 2+ 3+ 4+ 5+ Confident		____
Frustrated -5 -4 -3 -2 -1 <> 1+ 2+ 3+ 4+ 5+ Creativity		____
		TOTAL SCORE: ____

1. At work — Score _____

2. At home — Score _____

3. Personal relationships — Score _____

SOME QUESTIONS YOU CAN USE WITH YOUR SCORECARD

When you score high in one of the eight key attitudes:

1. How much of the time do you feel and think this way?

2. What are the thoughts and feelings that go along with these positive states?

3. How do you feel about yourself, others, the world?

4. When you are in a positive state of mind, what is your perspective on your past and your future? What reinforces or strengthens your positive qualities?

5. How can you pass on your positive attributes to others?

When you take the time to acknowledge your strengths and look at how you can enhance and pass them on, you will become even stronger and can create a positive environment around you. By being a role model and coaching and mentoring others in things that you excel at, you can broaden and deepen your experience and also be of service to others.

When you score low in one of the eight key attitudes:

1. How much of the time do you feel and think in this way?

2. What is the dialogue or commentary going on inside of your head?

3. What is the relationship between what you are thinking and what you are feeling?

4. What happened that triggered those thoughts for you? If you were to watch a typical sequence of your behavior that made you identify this attitude in slow motion, what might you notice?

5. What negative conclusions did you feel you were justified in making based on what was happening?

6. What might be other perspectives on the same event?

When you examine with a constructive eye those areas where you fall off your center, you will build the awareness that is necessary to make changes. It is important to have a neutral point of view when looking at your "negativities." So often you may want to outright reject, eliminate, and destroy negativities in yourself, but taking that approach only creates more negativity. Instead, you want to cultivate a true curiosity. If you can approach your negativities with a sense of curiosity instead of disdain, it will change your experience of them and allow for an opening to make a choice instead of a knee jerk reaction. This can be uncomfortable at first, but a few moments of discomfort can be the basis for making a change in your life that will eliminate this type of discomfort forever.

THE EVOLUTION OF IDEAS

The evolution of ideas and concepts through collaboration is a great process. I have been blessed to have amazing colleagues to work with and environments where we can freely bounce ideas off one another to manifest remarkable business and lifestyle results. I thank all the people who have enriched my growth and development along the way. The ideas presented in this book are the distillation of many disciplines, schools of thought, and individual contributions.

My personal awakening commenced while studying Zen Buddhism while I was a student at UC Davis. Part of the Zen training is working with a koan or phrase repeatedly until the mind transcends its normal functioning. While it is very difficult to describe entirely what happened one day while I was thinking about my koan (I was riding my bicycle in Davis, California, in the afternoon), it felt like the whole world as I knew it dropped away and I was in the middle of space with a matrix of golden orbs connected by golden strands of light. When my mind returned I was still riding my bike, but from that day forward the whole world was different. For years after that day many different insights have emerged about what that vision meant, and that experience is very much alive for me today.

While attending the University of California at Davis I met Jim Polidora, a professor who introduced me to the concept of mind-body, a revolutionary concept in 1975. I wrote an individual major in Psychophysiology at U.C. Davis out of my interest in the relationship between mind and body, then went on to study medicine at the Baylor College of Medicine P.A. Program, class of 1980. I practiced medicine as a P.A. at the Sacramento Preventive Medicine Clinic for five years. I learned much about how to use alternative therapies and patient empowerment to heal people.

I also was fortunate to study NeuroLinguistic Programming (NLP), a field of study created by Richard Bandler and John Grinder. NLP is a discipline that enables you to understand how you create your mental map of the world and how you can make changes to become more effective or happier at work or in life in general. After taking the basic course, I studied and was certified at the Master Practitioner level by Robert Dilts. Later I worked with Richard Bandler and was certified as one of his trainers for his programs. John Grinder served on my Ph.D. committee and assisted me in formulating the topic for my dissertation, NeuroSomatics.

1982 was a pivotal year that changed my life. I took an experiential workshop, The Sage Experience. I was so moved that I wrote a letter to the workshop leader, Brandon St. John, and told him I wanted to

learn to do what he did, to work with a large group of people and create a transformational experience for them. I met with him and he agreed to train me. I spent several weekends for about two years being his personal assistant, watching him do the seminar and learning from him how to lead the seminar. At the end of those two years Brandon passed away, and I ended up leaving my career in medicine to become one of the owners of the workshop company. Marilyn Atteberry, Brandon's business partner, and I reorganized the business and I began leading these personal development seminars in the U.S. and Europe.

While leading Sage in 1985 I met Vern Black, creator of the Integrity Tone Scale.[6] The Integrity Tone Scale was a complex chart that had sixteen different states of mind that Vern had devised along with suggestions on how to get out of negative states and get into positive states. One of the key points that Vern made was that "choosing" was the key to getting out of the drama cycle. This concept of choosing was a common theme in the work I was doing with the Sage Experience and from NeuroLinguistic Programming.

In working with Vern I began to think about how to simplify some of the elements of his model into a scheme that

---

[6] Vern Black, Handbook for the Integrity Tone Scale, Third Edition (San Francisco, California: Vern Black and Associates, 1984.

would be easier to teach in a business context. I had come up with a "Mind Map" chart that had nine states and made a visual logo, a scheme of two triangles, red and green, and a circle to represent the nine states.

INTEGRITY TONE SCALE

State of Integrity	Emotional Tone Scale	Attitude	Problem Recognition	Sulution (Love) Recognition	How to Move Out
Empower/Source	Serenity of Beingness Games Action	Serenity Ecstasy Joy Compassion	Liberty	Trust Faith	Expand Responsibility Increase Integrity Empower Others
Abundance	Exhilaration Aesthetic	Gratefulness Cherishing Ardor Enchantement	Welcome	Devotion	Economize Study for Even More Results Strengthen Elements That Cause Abundance
Normal	Enthusiasm Cheerfulness	Enthusiasm Admiration Cheerfulness	Opportunity	Enhancement	Strengthen Positive Results Adjust for Any Diminished Results
Emergency	Empathy Strong Interest	Amusement Liking Satisfaction Expectation	Challenge	Cooperation	Be at Purpose Promote Economize Prepare for Expanded Activity
Danger	Wondering Caution Mild Interest Concern Mild Anxiety	Curiosity	Lure	Discovery	Recognize Detrimental Elements and Handle Directly Insure Ethical Behavior
Non-Existence	Contented	Hope Distant	Feel Separated	Unimportant	Make Goal Locate Channels of Communication Communicate to Make Yourself Known Find Out What Is Needed or Wanted Start Doing It
Detriment/ Responsible	Disinterested Guilt Embarrassment Bored	Disappointment Disinterest Reluctance Self-consciousness Feeling Wrong Indifference Boredom	Obligation	Endeavor Assist Agree With	Clean Up Damage Acknowledge Your Trustworthiness List Your Valuablenesses Demonstrate Your Valuableness (Serve) Validate Your Accomplishment and Give Yourself a Gift
Uncertainty	Monotonous	Annoyance Vexation Exasperation	Infringement	Evasion Deflection	Choose
Adversary (Band #1)	Antagonism Hostility Pain	Defiance Shock Outrage Reasonableness	Attack	Suppression	Recognize Your Opposition to Results Discover Your Positions and Their Payoffs Choose to Play for Results
Adversary (Band #2)	Anger Hate	Arrogance Conceit Contempt	Insult	Dominance	
Disloyalty (Band #1)	Resentment No Sympathy Unexpressed Resentment Covert Hostility	Humiliation Resentment Petulance Sullenness Suspicion	Conspiracy	Stealth	Decide To Trust Yourself Tell the Truth About Your Experience List the Decisions to Trust Yourself
Disloyalty (Band #2)	Fear Despair Terror	Apprehension Fear Dread Worry	Threat	Protection	
Disloyalty (Band #3)	Numb Sympathy Propitiation	Loneliness Yearning Sympathy Propitiation Despondency Numbness	Trap	Rescue	
Disloyalty (Band #4)	Grief Making Amends Undeserving Self-Abasement Victim Hopeless				
Disloyalty (Band #5)	Apathy	Apathy	Overwhelm	Surrender	
Disloyalty (Band #6)	Useless Dying Failure Pity Regret Accountable Blame Shame Controlling Bodies Protecting Bodies Worshipping Bodies Sacrifice Hiding Being Objects Being Nothing Can't Hide Total Failure	Ruin Self Pity Blame Shame Condemned Greed Jealous Malice Anguish Nothing	Betrayal	Revenge	

MIND MAP

Paradigm	Operating Level	Perception	Meaning/Feeling	Decision/Belief	Behavior	Steps to Creating a Breakthrough
EMPOWERMENT	Vision	Appreciation Compassion Clarity — What is	Amusement Knowing Determined Grounded Humor	I am Commited I see the vision I Trust	Direct Receptive Compassion Open Coach Mentor	**Be Commited** Focus on your vision. See what is possible and enerate creative tension. Be a congruent example of living your values and principles. Mentor and coach. Expand responsibility. Encourage interdependance. Stay humble. Acknowledge diversity, appreciate and empower others. Keep a sense of humor.
	Strategy	Discovery	Confidence Enhancement Expansion	There is a clear path	Articulation Curiosity Learning Incorporation	**Be Focused & Enhance Everything** Optimize. Keep your mind open to continual cycles of learning. Economize but not wasting your energy. Do your internal and external house keeping. Acknowledge the excellence, knowledge, and mastery of others. Clarify your values, roles and principles.
	Inspiration	Welcome	Passion Grateful Wonder Hope Exhilarated	I see the Positive Intention You are a valuable contributor. We make it possible. I have Faith	Acknowledge Cooperation Opportunity	**Strategize** Establish your mission and purpose. Create context for service by identifying the activity that energizes you and results with a benefit for others. Step into the future of your goal completed. Look back & identify how you got there. What obstacles might you encounter? What are your assets and resources? Establish strategic partnerships. Prioritize. Move forward.
ACCOUNTABILITY	Responsibility 6	Anticipation	Mild Anxiety Risk Success/ Disappointment Satisfaction	Vitality Results Performance Sustaining	Vigilance Expectation	**Keep Agreements & Communicate** Identify and make important communications. Make explicit agreements that are critical to accomplish the goal. Hold yourself and other to account. Create feedback loops to keep things on target. Clean up damage from broken agreements and make new agreements. Develop expertise. Acknowledge success.
	Motivation 5	Challenge	Energized Vigor Assertive Anticipation Enthusiastic	I can / We can Lets go!	Action Team	**Take Action** Take the step forward to wad your goal. Asses the interim results and adjust accordingly. Align your activities, goals and relationships with your purpose. Develope your inner awareness to evaluate when you are off purpose. Be self correcting and open to input.
	Neutrality 4	Objective	Stability Tranquil	I can see both sides of the issue. I can freely choose. I am content	Independence	**Make Goals** Set a Specific, Measurable, Attainable, Meaningful, Time Bound Goal. Notice that neutrality is a foundation to build upon.
DRAMA	Uncertainty 3	Indecision	Confused Unbalanced Unstable	I don't know which one is "right."	Avoid	**Choose** Identify larger context. Remember you are always free to choose. Consider the future that each of your choices creates. Choose one and move into action. You can always re-choose.
	Adversary 2	I HAVE BEEN ATTACKED Assault	Frustrated Angry/Hostile Pain Reasonable Irritated Outrage	I'm right, You're wrong. I am shocked.	Attack/Defend Sarcasm Antagonize Insult Blame	**Go for Results** Stop defending yourself and blaming others. Stop trying to be right. Realize that you are opposing the results. Put your ears back on and listen to the others point of view. ASk, "What do you want?" Take a stand for their outcome. Identify and articulate your mutual positive outcomes.
	Victim 1	I HAVE BEEN BETRAYED Betrayal Threat	Fear Regret Apathy Humiliation Jealous Trap Burden Overwhelm	There is something wrong with me. You have power, I am powerless. I will get even.	Revenge Protection Stealth Control Rescue Consolation	**Tell the Truth** Realize that YOU have stopped believing in yourself. Separate what actually happened from what you made up about it. What were you afraid or assuming might be true about you? Do a reality check. Identify your positive aspects and strengths. Tell the truth to yourself and others about the drama that you created. Tell the truth about your positive value. Take a stand for yourself. Have no withholds. Acknowledge your positive attributes. Realize that your thoughts are creating your perception of reality.

FROM PERSONAL TRANSFORMATION TO BUSINESS TRANSFORMATION

As part of Sage, Marilyn Atteberry and I created an advanced training program called Warrior with Heart and offered a nine-day leadership program called Leaders with Heart. Many executives were going through the leadership program and requested to have a similar type of workshop offered inside of their businesses.

For the second five years that I owned Sage, I started focusing on doing business seminars. In 1995 I stopped leading Sage and sold the Sage franchise to a colleague in Germany and began doing business seminars exclusively.

In addition to running my own company and I formed partnerships with Charlotte Milliner, President of the Center for Professional Development, Charlie Sheppard, President of Management Communication Systems, and Stephen Xavier President of the Cornerstone Executive Development Group. I was leading corporate workshops, doing training and doing individual executive coaching, and this has been my career since 1995, doing executive development, team development, and organizational change initiatives.

For this book the intention is to take a different approach to presenting the concepts, tools, and ideas. This summer, while I was hiking in Yosemite with my daughter, the idea of mind molecules popped in my mind as the metaphor that I wanted to use. Not only did mind molecules fit with my background in science, medicine, and psychology, but it also reminded me of a movie, *What the Bleep Do You Know?* One point the movie makes is that our thoughts set up an internal chemistry in our bodies. If you get a chance to see the movie it also provides a refreshing look at how each of us creates our own reality. While the elements of classical leadership and drama molecules have six elements that seem to be inclusive, each person has the unique opportunity to create his/her individualized positive and negative molecules. It is important to take any model that you learn and personalize it so that it is uniquely yours. Allow the models that you learn in this book and in your life to inspire your creativity so that you can make them fit your own life.

As you approach the door to each experience in your life the challenge is to continually seek new ways to make choices so that you can be more productive, feel good, and create a positive environment for others at work and in your life overall.

"There must be a positive and negative in everything in the universe in order to complete a circuit or circle, without which there would be no activity, no motion."
—John McDonald